NEW
POEMS

#2

NEW
POEMS

BY AMERICAN POETS
#2

edited by Rolfe Humphries

Granger Index Reprint Series

BOOKS FOR LIBRARIES PRESS
FREEPORT, NEW YORK

"A Pavane for the Nursery," by William J. Smith, Copyright 1954 by *Accent*; "Saint Francis Borgia," by Phyllis McGinley appeared in *America* magazine; "Grisaille With a Spot of Red," by Samuel Yellen, copyright 1954 by *The Antioch Review*, Incorporated; "So Long, Folks, Off to the War," © 1954 by Anthony Ostroff, and "Song," © 1957 by Jan Burroway, appeared in *The Atlantic Monthly*; "The Unawkward Singers," by David Ferry, Copyright 1952 by *Audience*; "The Eyes of Children at the Brink of the Sea's Grasp," by Josephine Jacobsen, and "This Is Pioneer Weather," by William Carlos Williams, Copyright 1956 and 1957 by *The Beloit Poetry Journal*; "Weeping Willow," by Richard Aldridge, Copyright 1954 by *Chicago Review*; "maggie and milly and molly and may," Copyright 1956 by E. E. Cummings, "Where, When, Which," by Langston Hughes, and "To Flossie," by William Carlos Williams, appeared in *The Colorado Review*, the two last copyrighted 1956 and 1957 respectively by *The Colorado Review*; a different version of "Leaping Falls," by Galway Kinnell, appeared in *Conservative Review* under the title "Spicatto," Copyright 1957 by *Conservative Review*; "The Sensualists," by Theodore Roethke, and "i am a little church (no great cathedral)," Copyright 1957 by E. E. Cummings, appeared in *Encounter* (London); "I Knew a Woman," by Theodore Roethke, and "L'lle du Levant: The Nudist Colony," by Barbara Howes, appeared in *Harper's Bazaar*; "The River Glideth," Copyright © 1954 by Anthony Ostroff, appeared in *Harper's Magazine*; "Calypso" and "The Gift," by William Carlos Williams, Copyright 1957 by *The Hudson Review*, Inc.; "A Poor Relation," by Audrey McGaffin, "The Giraffe" and "The Vole," by Marvin Solomon, and "The Cloud of Unknowing," by Philip Murray, appeared in *Imagi*; "The Road," by Herbert Morris, appeared in *The Kenyon Review*, Copyright 1957 by Kenyon College; "On Being Invited to a Testimonial Dinner," by William Stafford, appeared in *Liberation*; "Incense," by Louise Townsend Nicholl, appeared in *Literary Review*, Copyright 1957 by Fairleigh Dickinson University; "The Sun Men Call It," by John Hall Wheelock, appeared in *The Lyric*, Copyright 1955 by Ruby Altizer Roberts; "A Time of Light, a Time of Shadow," by Samuel Yellen (1954), "The Chance," by John Holmes (1957), and "The Greater Music," by T. Weiss (1957), appeared in *The Nation* and were copyrighted in the respective years shown by The Nation Associates; "Catwise," by Philip Booth, and "The Locust Hunt," by Philip Murray, appeared in *The New Mexico Quarterly*, Copyright 1954 and 1956 respectively by The University of New Mexico; "Testimony to an Inquisitor," by William Stafford, appeared in *New Orleans Poetry Journal*; "What the Bones Know," by Carolyn Kizer (1955), "Shimmer of Evil," by Theodore Roethke (1955), "The Wit," by Elizabeth Bishop (1956) and "Sunday in the Country," by May Swenson (1956), appeared in *The New Republic* and were copyrighted in the respective years shown by *The New Republic*, Inc.; the following poems copyrighted by *The New Yorker* Magazine, Inc. in the years shown (respectively): "A Certain Age" and "Fourteenth Birthday" by Phyllis McGinley, "Colonel B" by Constance Carrier—1955; "Carry Me Back" by John Holmes and "Earliness at the Cape" by Babette Deutsch—1956; "March Twilight" and "The Meeting" by Louise Bogan, "Squatter's Children" by Elizabeth Bishop and "Two Voices in the Meadow" by Richard Wilbur—1957; "On the Way to the Island," by David Ferry, appeared in *Paris Review*; "Death of a Jazz Musician," by William J. Smith (1956), "Values in Use," by Marianne Moore (1956), and "Pangloss' Song," by Richard Wilbur (1957), appeared in *Partisan Review* and were copyrighted in the respective years shown by *Partisan Review*; "Morning Worship," by Mark Van Doren, Copyright 1957 by *Pax*; "Told by Seafarers," by Galway Kinnell and "The People at the Party," by Lisel Mueller, Copyright 1954 and 1957 respectively by *Perspective*; "July Dawn," by Louise Bogan, appeared in *Poems in Folio*; "Cold," by Robert Francis (1954), "The North of Wales" (1955), "Workmen" (1956), and "The Brahms" (1956), by Herbert Morris, and "New construction: Bath Iron Works," by Stanley Koehler (1957), appeared in *Poetry*, and were copyrighted in the respective years shown by Modern Poetry Association; "The Morning Porches," Copyright 1956 by Donald Hall, also appeared in *Poetry*; "The Middle Ages," by Leah Bodine Drake, and "The Hunter," by Eleanor Glenn Wallis, appeared in *Recurrence*, Copyright 1954 and 1956 respectively by Grover Jacoby; "The Seed Eaters" (1954) and "Boy Riding Forward Backward" (1956), by Robert Francis, "Advice to Travelers," by Walker Gibson (1956), Epigram No. 4 by Donald Hall (1957), and "Sans Souci," by Lisel Mueller (1957), appeared in *Saturday Review* and were copyrighted in the respective years shown by Saturday Review Associates, Inc.; "The Triumph of Chastity" and "The Triumph of Death," by Barbara Howes, appeared in *The Sewanee Review*; "The Beautiful Horses," by Donald Hall, copyright 1956 by *Shenandoah*; "The Wood of the Self-destroyers," by Samuel Yellen, appeared in *Southwest Review*, © 1956 by Southern Methodist University Press; "Apples," by Lisel Mueller, and Epigrams 1, 2, and 3 by Donald Hall, Copyright 1957 by *Talisman*; "Dead Snake," by William J. Smith (1954), "In a City Square," by Eleanor Glenn Wallis (1956), "Short, Short Story," by Josephine Jacobsen (1957), and "The Cemetery Is," by Audrey McGaffin (1957), appeared in *Voices* and were copyrighted in the respective years shown by Harold Vinal; "Outside," by William Stafford (1954), "The Centaur," by May Swenson (1956), and "To the Western World," by Louis Simpson (1957), appeared in *The*

STANDARD BOOK NUMBER:
8369-6165-X

LIBRARY OF CONGRESS CATALOG CARD NUMBER:
70-121924

MANUFACTURED BY
HALLMARK LITHOGRAPHERS, INC.
IN THE U.S.A.

INTRODUCTION

All the material from which these two-hundred-odd poems were selected came to us directly from the poets themselves. Their responses, warm and gratifying, answered the letters we sent to the contributors to our first *New Poems* and to as many others as we could reach. Paul Engle kindly mentioned our project in his Iowa Poetry Workshop; friends passed the word along to other friends. The announcement in *Poetry* brought the number of poems submitted to over two hundred a week; and *The New York Times'* notice more than doubled the tally. Truly, an embarrassment of riches.

Our apologies to our former contributors, who are so stingily represented here. They were, and are, a goodly company. Since 1953, when our first collection appeared (we do not claim *Post hoc, ergo propter hoc*) every major prize for American poetry—The Academy of American Poets Fellowship, the Bollingen, the Pulitzer, the National Book Award—has fallen to the lot of one or another, as our biographies here show; and besides these prizes, there have been other awards and fellowships too numerous to mention. Seven of those contributors have, since 1953, published first books; two of these, by Philip Booth and Constance Carrier, won the Lamont awards. (The other Lamont winner, Donald Hall, is represented in this collection.) We have both hope and confidence that in the next five years more winners, now making their first appearance, will emerge; as they say at the race track, tab the following as among those likely to get the job done—Robert Bagg, Jan Burroway, David Ferry, George Garrett, Kim Kurt, Herbert Morris, Lisel Mueller, Anthony Ostroff, Charles David Webb.

During the last month of preparing this book, our conscience became greatly troubled. We learned, to our sorrow, that we could not possibly use, in our allotted pages, all the good poems that were coming in; to return them was grievous indeed. If we say, "This hurts us more than it does you," we hope it will not be taken for cant. We gladly pass on to the reader the advice to keep his eyes open for work by Bruce Berlind, G. P. Elliott, Robert Krieger, Douglas Nichols, Kenneth Pitchford, Sheila Pritchard, William Snodgrass (who made use of his own name in a poem with the refrain "Snodgrass is walking through the universe"), Louis Stanley, and Robert Tucker. Some of these have had considerable publication; others have yet to make their first appearance in print. In our book we have tried to keep the same balance, presenting both a substantial body of work hitherto unpublished, and at the same time recognizing that which has appeared, particularly in the smaller magazines which perform a yeoman service at considerable cost. This book makes no pretense to being a definitive selection; it is a random sampling, rather, of what goes on in American poetry today.

What does go on? Having been exposed to this quantity of material, an editor should presumably be qualified to proclaim Certain Significant Trends. I doubt that the evidence is really sufficient for sound conclusions, but will nevertheless venture a few remarks. For one thing, the obscure and the minatory, which E. M. Forster, less than a decade ago, considered the characteristic stigmata of modern poetry, seem to be disappearing. There are not nearly as many atom-bomb, or "I feel terrible," pieces as there were last time. For another thing, we have considerable return to form, not always, to be sure, fully realized; blank verse, the beat of iambic pentameter, takes over from the Amy Lowell type free verse. And I have seen, this time, scores of sestinas and villanelles.

In his introduction to the recent Faber & Faber anthology of modern American poetry, Mr. W. H. Auden, after announcing boldly that Americans differ much more *inter se* than do the British, corrects himself in a footnote and notes what he calls the beginning of a disturbing tendency for everybody to write alike. I do not think this is necessarily a bad sign: everybody, more or less, wrote alike in the days of the Elizabethans, and in the age of Pope. Can you, gentle reader, unless you happen to know the particular poem, distinguish a Drayton from a Daniel, or a Tate from a Johnson? The common characteristics of mid-twentieth century verse in America are somewhat harder to define than those of the periods mentioned above, but I think I agree with Mr. Auden's idea, and believe I can (sometimes without even opening the envelopes) recognize, if not define, its traits. The poems he speaks of, (or the kind of poetry he means,) use a common idiom, rather consciously literary, very competently turned, showing considerable evidence of serious study of technique (though the application may sometimes be grievously faulty), interested in observation almost to the point of catalogue, and withal rather noncommittal in spirit, not very reckless, just a bit chill, as if hedged with a cold war play-it-pretty-safe-brother kind of injunction.

This is the kind of verse that more than any other finds

fashionable acceptance. Editors have little to worry about if they print it. Yet more than this goes on; if we are, on the surface, developing a common manner, underneath that surface we are also preparing, and practicing, the break-through, the antithesis to that thesis. The voice of the individual, however isolated, however unpaid, speaks out in its own manner; there are people, still, who are not afraid of being themselves. (There are also those who are too damn proud of it, but that is another story.) We have some of them in this book; their range geographically is from coast to coast, chronologically from septuagenarians to those barely out of their teens. We are grateful to them, happy to present them to you; we hope you will like them, and tell them so.

ROLFE HUMPHRIES

New York City
June, 1957

Contents

SAMUEL L. ALBERT

All of Her

I did not come to kiss her for she was kiss herself;
Nor did I come to love her, love was hers as well.
I came to hold her hand and nest it by the sea.
For she was all I had and that's all there was of me.

I did not come to seize her, she was chains of steel;
Nor did I come to speak to her, her voice a liquid smile.
I came to hold her hand, and nest it by the sea.
For I was all of her, and she was all of me.

One, Two, Three

Fog got him first
As he wheeled around the bend
And slanted toward the valley.

It moved in fast
Embracing the car wholly
And everything else surely.

Fear got him second
As he dared not continue on
Nor stop for what might be in back.

Fate got him third
As thunder on huge tires roared in
And hurtled him into space forever.

Street-Walker in March

This is a night to be out
Whoring with the wind.
Tippling with her spring draughts
Beguiling to her secret bower,
Your head upon her breast.

1

Her moistened lips seeking
Your mouth; slapping your face
With the back of her hand.

Her strident limbs buckling
Around your waist, combing
Your hair with caressing fingers.

This is a night to be out
Whoring with the wind.

Rebuff

If you'd rather not to kiss then say so then
I would not unfair thee well against thy will.
Thou whom the gods made so short a time ago
Need not concern thyself, but save.

Who will watch thee grow, else from these dark eyes,
And wander through the fields again and soon
Shaping thy life, thy walk, thy hair a thousand;
And turn thee which way whatsoever so often?

Who in thy high hour and thy low ebb
Will awaken at night and listen acutely,
Gleaning the slightest refractory gaze or breeze,
Tilting its marginal way so this, so that?

If you'd rather not to kiss then say so then.
Wander out the dark the distant way.
One more less a guiding hand and star,
Alone and pitched the desert path and gone.

Near the Base Line

I saw death this afternoon lurking near the tennis courts;
The balls flailing the air and the sun in highest fever.
The struggling youth no longer turned to when he was a boy
But smote and belt as if turning man himself away.

In the shade and quiet of the after game, the sweat pouring
    down and ceasing,
A coolness came upon him and there was no singing.
Across, the sun splashed a foot thick glare
And men were desperate to recapture their madness.

2

Is it the fuzziness and new of the tennis ball they seek;
The mystery of that far corner shot for which there is no
    return?
Is the touch of God in the ace across the net spewing the
    chalk away.
The echo of Neanderthal in the reckless stretch to retrieve
    and conquer?

I do not know, but men will come again to play;
Their bones a pitying opponent for so stern a foe.
And while the solid sun and thwack will know the challenge,
Death will be lurking near the base lines.

After a Game of Squash

And I thought of how impossibly alone we were,
Up in the room where the lockers are and the showers.
He with wiping the sweat from his face and head
And I bending over, loosening the laces from my sneakers.

We had just finished this long game of squash.
Then, we were much closer; smashing the same ball;
Lurching forward, out-maneuvering each other
Hard down the sidelines, death to the opponent.

It was a battle, the killer's eye in the middle
Of the round black ball. Two men struggling
To find each other out. What made each one's mind work
And with what heart each fell to the long odds.

And when the game was over we thanked each other gen-
    erously;
Complimented one the other on his skill, his finesse.
And I thought of how impossibly alone we were,
Up in the room where the lockers are and the showers.

SAMUEL L. ALBERT, *born in Boston, Mass., in 1911, graduated from Harvard in 1934. Father of five sons, he lists his vocation as General Agent for the Washington National Insurance Company, and in his leisure he enjoys playing tennis and taking long walks. He makes his home in Newton Center, Mass. These are his first published poems.*

3

RICHARD ALDRIDGE

A Serendipity of Love

The day's swim done, we found some grass and flung
Ourselves down side by side next to the pool.
The sun was old, with shadows leaning long.
What speech we made was low and casual
Yet sounded to my ears as though we sang,
Since every word was one more spoon of soil
Thrown on the weeks-old grave of love gone wrong.

Until, to have a change, she sat up straight
But turned to let her gaze descend to mine.
Unasked, she edged a little to the right
To put her head between me and the sun.
A minute passed before I noticed that,
Arranged so, round her unkempt hair there shone
A perfect halo of rich golden light.

By Return Mail
(upon being reprimanded for a pleonasm)

When there was not one moment left to us
The pilot watched us kiss goodbye (I saw
Him look away when you had turned to go);
Then, easily as taffy pulls apart
I stood as you were flown into the maw
Of summer sky that swallowed you. And so
I walked back where we'd walked, got on a bus
And came directly home with ashen heart.

That night I wrote to you, I guess too soon,
Because the famous futile line crept in
That runs 'I can't think of much more to say'
(For if I can't I shouldn't, hm?). I meant,
Though, something rather more: you know the way
A child with head bent back sees his balloon
That slipped out of his grasp by accident
Grow smaller like the disappearing jinn?

4

It vanishes at last, and in his head
The old words used for loss have vanished too.
I felt like that as I had felt before
When your eyes spoke of possibility
I'd put away long since as nothing more
Than dreams—no words to say what can't be said.
Being so completely lost in love with you
I send this verse along to make you see.

Weeping Willow

Cascading streamers down of palest green
The weeping willow stands quite motionless, as though
Herself incredulous of her own lovely mien;
    Resplendent here in her first, rare springtime leaf
As the flung white burst after breakers hit a reef
    That plunges surely down, all shimmering and slow.

Is, then, this paragon of symbols meant
To seem the tears of all the ages, loosed to flow
As freely as her own fountain-like descent?
    She stands demure and grave, a queen-like Sphinx
Who knows far more of grief than tears. Her silence links
    Three thousand years, recalling long ago

A woman standing lone against the sky,
Arms folded on her breast, long dress hung full and still,
Whose gaze sought out a further thing than other eye
    Could see or guess. An hour each day she waited there
Until at last, without a sound, she'd smooth her hair,
    And drop her eyes, and turn home down the hill.

RICHARD ALDRIDGE, *born in New York City in 1930, is a graduate of Amherst College. He served in the army for two years with the Counter-Intelligence Corps, and has spent two years at Oxford on a Fulbright Scholarship, earning his degree in the Honour School of English Language and Literature. His first book of poems, entitled* An Apology Both Ways, *will appear this year.*

W. H. AUDEN

There Will Be No Peace

Though mild clear weather
Smile again on the shire of your esteem,
And its colors come back, the storm has changed you:
    You will not forget, ever,
The darkness blotting out hope, the gale
    Prophesying your downfall.

You must live with your knowledge:
Way back, beyond, outside of you are others
In moonless absences you never heard of,
    Who have certainly heard of you,
Beings of unknown number and gender,
    And they do not like you.

What have you done to them?
Nothing? Nothing is not an answer:
You will find yourself thinking—how can you help it?—
    That you did, you did do something;
You will find yourself wishing you could make them laugh,
    You will long for their friendship.

There will be no peace:
Fight back, then, with such courage as you have
And every unchivalrous dodge you know of,
    Clear in your conscience on this;
Their cause, if they had one, is nothing to them now,
    They hate for hate's sake.

First Things First

Woken, I lay in the arms of my own warmth and listened
To a storm enjoying its storminess in the winter dark
Till my ear, as it can when half-asleep or half-sober,
Set to work to unscramble that interjectory uproar,
Construing its airy vowels and watery consonants
Into a love-speech indicative of a proper name.

Scarcely the tongue I should have chosen yet, so far
As harshness and clumsiness would allow, it spoke in your
    praise,
Kenning you a godchild of the Moon and the West Wind
With power to tame both real and imaginary monsters,
Likening your poise of being to an upland county,
Here green on purpose, there pure blue for luck.

Loud though it was, alone as it certainly found me,
It reconstructed a day of peculiar silence
When a sneeze could be heard a mile off, and had me
    walking
On a headland of lava beside you, the occasion as ageless
As the stare of any rose, your presence exactly
So once, so valuable, so very now.

This, moreover, at an hour when only too often
A smirking devil annoys me in beautiful English,
Predicting a world where every sacred location
Is a sand-buried site all cultured Texans 'do,'
Misinformed and thoroughly fleeced by their guides,
And gentle hearts are extinct like Hegelian bishops.

Grateful, I slept till a morning that would not say
How much it believed of what I said the storm had said,
But quietly drew my attention to what had been done,
— So many cubic meters the more in my cistern
Against a leonine summer — putting first things first:
Thousands have lived without love, not one without water.

Objects

All that which lies outside our sort of why,
Those wordless creatures who are there as well,
Remote from mourning yet in sight and cry,
Make time more golden than we meant to tell.

Tearless, their surfaces appear as deep
As any longing we believe we had;
If shapes can so to their own edges keep,
No separation proves a being bad.

There is less grief than wonder on the whole
Even at sunset though, of course, we care
Each time the same old shadow falls across

One person who is not. Somewhere a soul,
Light in her bestial substance, well aware,
Extols the silence of how soon a loss.

The Island Cemetery

This grave-yard with its umbrella pines
Is inferior in status to our vines,
And though more guests keep crowding in
Must stay the size it's always been.

Where lives are many, acres few,
The dead must be cultivated too,
Like seeds in any farmer's field
Are planted for the bones they yield.

It takes about eighteen months for one
To ripen into a skeleton,
To be washed, then folded, packed in a small
Niche hollowed out of the cemetery wall.

Curiosity made me stop
While sextons were digging up a crop:
Why should bards so take it amiss
That Alexanders come to this?

Wherever our personalities go,
(And, to tell the truth, we do not know),
The solid structures they leave behind
Are no discredit to our kind.

Mourners may miss, and they do, a face,
But at least they cannot detect a trace
Of those fish-like hungers, mammalian heats,
That kin our flesh to the coarser meats.

And who would be ashamed to own
To a patience that we share with stone,
This underlying thing in us
Which never at any time made a fuss?

Considering what our motives are,
We ought to thank our lucky star
That Love must ride to reach his ends
A mount that has no need of friends.

Song

So large a morning, so itself, to lean
Over so many and such little hills,
All at rest in roundness and rigs of green,
Can cope with this rebellious wing that wills
To better its obedient double quite
As daring in the lap of any lake,
The wind from which ascension puts to flight
Tribes of a beauty that no care can break.
Climbing to song it hopes to make amends
For whiteness drabbed, for glory said away
And be immortal after but because
Light upon a valley where its love was
So lacks all picture of reproach it ends
Denying what it started up to say.

W. H. AUDEN, *now Professor of Poetry at the University of Oxford, was born in York, England, in 1907. Author of numerous books of poetry, including* The Age of Anxiety *(which won him the Pulitzer Prize),* Nones, *and* The Shield of Achilles, *he collaborated with Chester Kallman on the libretto for the Stravinsky opera,* The Rake's Progress, *and has been editor of many volumes, the latest an anthology of American poetry. He is a member of the American Academy of Arts and Letters.*

DONALD C. BABCOCK

Meditation By Mascoma Lake
(1917)

Peace lies profound on these forgotten acres.
The hayfield is unkempt and gone to weed,
And so are they who lived by their strange creed,
Who built stone barns and called themselves the Shakers.

In the great chestnut tree the wild bees hum;
Feebly the water laps the pebbled shore;
Of all that old apocalyptic lore
This languid midday moment is the sum.

They would create no thing. Though willing makers
Of honest artless wares and homespun, yet
They scorned alike to bear and to beget:
Peace lies profound on their forgotten acres.

". . . Discourse Heard One Day . . ."

". . . and one of these is Love . . ." (Diotima)

". . . but the greatest of these is Love." (St. Paul)

Ageless, the Mantinean woman speaks,
And we, who think great Socrates remote,
And Plato one we know not, though we quote,
Find her the wisest Sibyl of the Greeks.
Hers is the word that every votary seeks:
Time's long diminuendo leaves this note
To vibrate like the veery's song and float
Among the meditative mountain peaks.
Now comes a hush upon the Banquet Hall,
And quiet grows the long Symposium:
On tiptoe by the door, against the wall,
The wise of yesteryear expectant come,
While he of Tarsus marks the word she said,
And, gravely acquiescent, bows his head.

10

Adios

Autumn is for older men
Meekly to become again
Irresponsible among
Those who busily walk young,
Those who manage great affairs,
Those who run upon the stairs.

Old men need not have a goal.
Casual at noon they stroll,
Cogitating nothing vaster
Than the lone bee on the aster—
Pondering in the afternoon
The uncommunicative moon,
Which itself in ponderous poise
Hangs beyond the reach of noise—
Musing, when the shadows fall,
Over things beyond recall—
Knowing, in the deep of night,
The hour's unpunctuated flight,
Hearing faint the far-off mirth
Of ages moving up to birth.

Autumn tells the older man
There is nothing more to plan—
Nought for him, except to say:
God abide the coming day!

DONALD C. BABCOCK *was born in Minneapolis, Minn., in 1885. He has published* Man and Social Achievement, *a study of social evolution, and won the Durham Poetry Award, given by the University of New Hampshire Writers' Conference, for his brochure,* For Those I Taught. *A volume of poems,* New England Harvest, *was published in 1953. Mr. Babcock is Professor Emeritus of Philosophy at the University of New Hampshire, and lives in Durham, N. H.*

ROBERT BAGG

For Her on the First Day Out

Let no pirate's sword storm these veins of yours,
Let no other hands haul the blossom of your blouse full sail,
Let no other sailor ride the ship in its sinking,
No other helmsman whistle the wind so your hair flails,

Let none but these arms hold you close to the wind
As the wind rises and the ship sinks in its own wake.
Let none but the drowned man make peace with your wild
    waves,
Listening to your white hair wailing for the sea's dark sake.

Speak This Kindly to Her

The final secret that two lovers shared,
Their falling out of love, they kept for days,
Knowing how previous farewells had fared.

Just being patient would not work always,
She said. That took time, and time was better used.
Often, completion of a passionate phrase

Lapsed into breath. Seldom were their eyes fused
For sharing certain delicate excitements.
And they were neither soulful nor amused

When conversations gossiped in past tense
About two lovers who quarreled, a lively pair.
Their own love stung a little in that presence.

"The old curl-less way, that's how I loved your hair."
"Your careless praise for it was my first despair."

Ballad in Blonde Hair Foretold

The crow lies over the cornfield,
The sun flies over the crow,
The crow will fall on the corn,
And sun will light on the crow.

Fishermen find the water
A surface of sad smooth sounds.
I fished the surf for a sad sad man,
Now he is only sound.

I cleaned his brow of salt and time
With hands of river water,
I wish his laugh and luck
Would never run like water.

"Aha" he said, "A glimpse of your hair
Sends shivers throughout the sun.
I swam through death and drenched I rose,
But I will dry in the sun."

With bird-sharp eyes he whistled me,
Tossed me like grain at the breeze.
The sun sets over his shoulder,
His words go by on the breeze.

The crow lies over the cornfield,
The sun flies over the crow,
The crow will light on the corn,
And sun will fall on the crow.

Fishermen find the water
A surface of sad smooth sounds.
I fished the surf for a sad sad man.
Now he is only sound.

Oracle at Delphi

King Croesus carried to Apollo's sibyl
    Gifts golden to the core,
Infallible gold shining as her syllables
    Shone: Croesus was fully aware
Truth came highly priced and hard, like war.

He was nervous when she whispered to the god,
    Fumes clouded what he came for.
Blood dozed as his veins inhaled what she said:
    Strike Persia with this war
And dark tears will dry on a dazzling Empire.

Exultant Croesus swung her prophecies
    Like tongue-sharp flanges on his ax.
Enemies toppled to its truth like lies.
    (O Croesus, you were lax
To trust your faulty grasp of Grecian syntax.)

That morning all the baffling lines of battle
    Joined like a palindrome.
Reading left he saw his veterans ripple
    Forward like ranks of sea spume,
Then reading right saw his cavalry crumple.

He heard the laugh of triumph split both flanks
    To hideous confusion.
Valor filled every other heart, and thanks
    Poured from alternate wounds.
Joy and destruction melted in the sun.

The tide of battle turned in his stomach.
    Her undigested words
Lunged out his throat, but he couldn't vomit Luck
    Which through his rich veins toured
Like a gay poison. When she at last got bored

With flushing false glory through Croesus' organs,
    Her truth began to squeeze
His cold sweat out, and water his commands
    With fear. He saw his armies
Stream from skirmishes like tears from stinging eyes.

In such stampedes, sounding kingdoms have fallen,
    Leaving behind a hush
Piled like thunder. Croesus watched with appalling
    Trust, air draining clear at last.
There lay his coruscating armies, crushed,

As twilight looted their magnificence.
    Annihilation seemed a lull
In the battle, his ruin made slow sense:
    He felt the oracle's
Imaginary sentence from which bronze nouns fall.

These battles, betrayals, deaths, are foolish gold
    Flaming in the coffers
Of her prophecies. Her words stand like moulds,
    His fortunes boil and blur,
Then freeze to strong bronze deeds no singing stirs.

He might have preferred a less hardened death:
    A lion falling like lightning,
Paws spinning the earth, devouring a path
    To his throat, claws alighting
Sleekly, so blood ran like hot gold in his mouth.

ROBERT BAGG *was born in Orange, N. J., in 1935 and was graduated from Amherst in 1957* cum laude. *While an undergraduate he edited the* Amherst Literary Magazine, *won several poetry prizes, and published poems in* Poetry, Semicolon, *and* The Atlantic Monthly. *Amherst has awarded him a special Simpson Fellowship in honor of Robert Frost to spend a year writing in Europe.*

ELIZABETH BARTLETT

The Cage

Thoughts like an empty cage
Receive the morning
Through the windowpane
And quietly swing

No flutter brings my eye
To a meaninged core
For the waking light
The door transparent

Held blind by the mirror
And deaf by the bell
I must search my mind
By taste, smell and touch

Bars silhouette a wall
To enclose the noon
Where images halt
And the night soon comes

Oh bird that set me free
To try my own wings
How this false spring tree
Clings that I perch on

The Question Is Proof

If I ask why
You need not reply
The question is proof

Only my ear
Can help me to hear
The rain on the roof

What thoughts I own
Are shaped by my bone
And etched on my brain

Nothing more real
Than the moods I feel
And what they explain

Warm hands or cold
The world that I hold
Is all I can show

The more or less
I measure by guess
Is all that I know

All that I see
With my eye is me
And no other truth

Here with my feet
Time walks on the street
In age as in youth

Unless you lie
In asking why
You have the reply

Behold This Dreamer

He who would climb the heights of tone
And scale the peaks beyond the listening ear
Must first walk over water
And learn to stand on air, alone.

He who would swim the waves of light
And dive past shores into a sunless glow
Must first merge with his shadow
And melt through solid glass, like night.

Where eyes are fins and sound is leap
The rhythmic force performs its own ballet,
When dreams are fired in clay
They burn a path through timeless sleep.

17

Dark Angel

Dark angel of the night, you come on folded wings
Secret and silent, bringing sleep. To you belong
The rosemary and poppy, the longed for dream
From which the road turned in its lost beginning.

You have seen the frightened eyes of the city glow
From the Thames, Montmartre and the roofs of Moscow,
And you know how small a kilowatt burns in each
Single, separate room and how each one reaches
At last a diminishing point beyond which none
Can see but you. Night is your hour and with it comes

The inevitable surrender, peaceful or
With clash of arms, with unfulfilled hopes, terrors,
The fingers still clutching at the vanishing day,
The throat strangled by the unuttered word it says,
The ear straining for the unheard response, the thought
Immense in the dark. Only you, dark angel, born

Of our love and pity, speed night's passing feet
Around the earth, on rotating centuries
Across the stars, journeying over the ruins
Of forgotten time since you first left that home
Where the dream began, where the road turned and the sun
Swung in its orbit, bringing you, dark angel, down.

ELIZABETH BARTLETT, *born in New York City, has been a
teacher, book reviewer, lecturer, and writer. Her first collection,*
poems of yes and no, *was published in 1952; the above
poems are part of her second,* Until Words Cease. *Her work has
appeared in the* Beloit Poetry Journal, Harper's Magazine,
Harper's Bazaar, The Saturday Review, *and in many literary
quarterlies. Married to artist-writer Paul Bartlett, she now lives
in Atlanta, Ga., having recently returned from Yucatan,
Mexico.*

18

CHARLES G. BELL

Termites

A friend writes me from the temperate zone:
He has a fourth child, a gold-haired girl.
Here the termites are swarming.
Through unscreened windows
They drift in whirls to the light.
Dropping wings,
Pale worms on the table,
They pursue and mate; then eat
Into the books, blotting the word.
Procreation wraps us like a spider's web.
How shall I write my friend blessings of the occasion
From this hot land where breeding is a curse?

Island Dogs

The island crawls with dogs; scrawny couples
Make bookends in the streets and the swagged bitches
With bone-bare ribs drop brown litters,
Give suck a while from dugs like tumors,

Then stagger off with prolapsed parts;
The pups beg from house to house,
Till garbage grown, with a mate as lean,
They make bookends. And nobody minds

(Tender-hearted!), except the impersonal law,
Having some modern crotchets half-digested,
From time to time gives obvious strays
A pellet of beef with a heart of poison.

In the name of health the poisoned wander.
But O the dog days of stinking heat
On the heels of the law, when the blown corpses
Lie in the street and flies quicken.

So health is guarded. But there remain
Chosen remnants, drab as the dead,
To beg and steal, to make bookends—
The old succession; run it again . . .

This is the character of returning dawn,
The way of earth and earth's exploded star,
Islands in space and sea and air,
All breeding places of the flesh we are.

Girl Walking

Here comes a girl so damned shapely
Loungers stop breathing. Conceive how subtly
She works those hips. She is all sex; she knows it.
Lace shows the bubs; she is proud of notice;
Head high, back arched, long braids, wide crupper,
She walks like dancing, calls the gods to tup her.

Her mother goes before, as broad as tall,
A moving hill of flesh, a breeding sack,
Swollen with stoking of all appetites.
She stirs her buttocks too, but not to our delight.

Sweet amorous girl, how can you stroll
With such impulsive beauty, admired by all,
Your destiny waddling before you down the road?

Banana

From the tattered banana tree after months of waiting,
In the rainless air before the spring rains came,
In the promise only of the moist coming,

Unexpectedly, from the highest shoot, a huge
Thing detached itself, leaving the sheath
Slowly, like a stallion's appalling member,

Curving, purpling, thrusting out an emergent
Flower, that lifted day by day, petals
Like loin cloths, revealing the genitalia—

Enlarging fingers of banana capped with bloom,
Dropping nectar, to which the small queen birds fly,

Converting (even as we, the lusts of flesh) into song
The shocking abandon of fertile and phallic bloom.

Love in Age

We shall have music
In the songless land:

20

All brown October
Hand in hand

Two go walking
The scrubby wood;
Idle talk
Common mood

Break in silence—
Have you heard?
Not a song, not a word,
With the ear nothing;

But hand in hand
All fall we go
In music through
The songless land.

Windowed Habitations

Looking over the water shows nothing but trees,
Green-shadowing nature. At sunset, suddenly,
A light appears: a torch, a star—O more:
Another sun—beautiful, blinding radiance
Pouring through dark leaves. It is only a reflection
From the world's light, now declined to its setting.
Behind that web of foliage is somebody's home,
Some windowed habitation, and from its panes,
Catching the sky's light, this light appears.
We are leaf-shadowed here; give us reflections,
Something of yours to image, that over the water,
Blinded, seeing through dark foliage the gold light pouring,
Someone off westward may say: "Ah, what a flashing. Surely
That is one of the soul's windowed habitations."

CHARLES G. BELL, *born in Greenville, Miss., in 1916, has been a Rhodes Scholar, a teacher at Princeton and Chicago Universities, and is now a tutor at St. John's College in Annapolis, Md. He has published two volumes of poems,* Songs for a New America *and* Delta Return. *Mr. Bell has also published articles on philosophical, literary, and political topics, and is at present working on a three-volume cultural history,* Spirit Takes Form, *an organic study of the Western arts.*

21

Squatter's Children

On the unbreathing sides of hills
they play, a specklike girl and boy,
alone, but near a specklike house.
The sun's suspended eye
blinks casually, and then they wade
gigantic waves of light and shade.
A dancing yellow spot, a pup,
attends them. Clouds are piling up;

a storm piles up behind the house.
The children play at digging holes.
The ground is hard; they try to use
one of their father's tools,
a mattock with a broken haft
the two of them can scarcely lift.
It drops and clangs. Their laughter spreads
effulgence in the thunderheads,

weak flashes of inquiry
direct as is the puppy's bark.
But to their little, soluble,
unwarrantable ark,
apparently the rain's reply
consists of echolalia,
and Mother's voice, ugly as sin,
keeps calling to them to come in.

Children, the threshold of the storm
has slid beneath your muddy shoes;
wet and beguiled, you stand among
the mansions you may choose
out of a bigger house than yours,
whose lawfulness endures.
Its soggy documents retain
your rights in rooms of falling rain.

The Wit

"Wait. Let me think a minute," you said.
And in the minute we saw:
Eve and Newton with an apple apiece,
and Moses with the Law,
Socrates, who scratched his curly head,
and many more from Greece,
all coming hurrying up to now,
bid by your crinkled brow.

But then you made a brilliant pun.
We gave a thunderclap of laughter.
Flustered, your helpers vanished one by one;
and through the conversational spaces, after,
we caught—back, back, far, far—
the glinting birthday of a fractious star.

ELIZABETH BISHOP *was born in Massachusetts in 1911, graduated from Vassar College, and now makes her home in Brazil. She has published two books of poems,* North & South *(1946)* and Poems *(1955). She has been awarded Guggenheim and Partisan Review Fellowships, was Consultant in Poetry at the Library of Congress 1949-50, and received the Pulitzer Prize in 1956.*

March Twilight

This light is loss backward; delight by hurt and by bias
    gained;
Nothing we know about and all that we shan't have.
It is the light which presages to the loser luck,
And cowardice to the brave.

The hour when the oldest and the newest thoughts begin;
Light shed for the most desperate and kindest embrace.
A watcher in these new, late beams might well see another
    face
And look into Time's eye, as into a strange house, for what
    lies within.

July Dawn

It was a waning crescent
Dark on the wrong side
On which one does not wish
Setting in the hour before daylight
For my sleepless eyes to look at.

O, as a symbol of dis-hope
Over the July fields,
Dissolving, waning,
In spite of its sickle shape.

I saw it and thought it new
In that short moment
That makes all symbols lucky
Before we read them rightly.

Down to the dark it swam,
Down to the dark it moved,
Swift to that cluster of evenings
When curved toward the full it sharpens.

24

The Meeting

For years I thought I knew, at the bottom of the dream,
Who spoke but to say farewell,
Whose smile dissolved, after his first words
Gentle and plausible.

Each time I found him, it was always the same:
Recognition and surprise,
And then the silence, after the first words,
And the shifting of the eyes.

Then the moment when he had nothing to say
And only smiled again,
But this time toward a place beyond me, where I could not
 stay—
No world of men.

Now I am not sure. Who are you? Who have you been?
Why do our paths cross?
At the deepest bottom of the dream you are let in,
A symbol of loss.

Eye to eye we look, and we greet each other
Like friends from the same land.
Bitter compliance! Like a faithless brother
You take and drop my hand.

LOUISE BOGAN, *born in Livermore Falls, Me., in 1897, is the author of four books of poetry, the latest of which are* The Sleeping Fury *and* Poems and New Poems. *She has also published a work of prose criticism,* Achievement in American Poetry, 1900-1950. *Winner of numerous prizes, twice holder of a Guggenheim Fellowship, Miss Bogan was awarded the Bollingen Prize in 1955, and an honorary Litt. D. from the Western College for Women in Oxford, Ohio, in 1956. She has been appointed Visiting Lecturer at the Salzburg Seminar in Austria, for 1958.*

Animal Fair

Until I was a roustabout
around a one ring Big Top,
what I knew of animals
was not where their manure falls;
but when I rolled the sidewalls wrong
and folded in much camel dung,
I saw the owner of the circus field,
his farmer's eyes (as wide and wild
as children's) set on elephants
and hippopotami: great tenants
worth their weight to the scene
they leave so green, so jungle green.

Catwise

Coming out from a movie,
take (improbably)
a tiger cat, asleep
on the hood of your car:
in anger name him a name,
or hug him in your wonder;
whether you play St. Francis
or tail him like Huck Finn
is, catwise, much the same.
But always his tiger eye
projects its opal icon
on some memorial screen:
a sequence from the preview
to which you are going,
the dumbshow out of which
(humanly) you have come.

The Turning

It softens now. April snow
sinks melting in the lawn, the swamp
is blurred with promises, the willow
hazed faint green. A month ago

the view was longer. Through the fence,
by a last birch hung with ice-glazed
bittersweet, two cock pheasants
fed and risked their iridescence.

Faced with snow, and a North wind,
no bird or woodlot animal owns
protective color, nor does a mind
that hunts the contrasts of this land

when its cold distances freeze clear.
It softens now. The frozen rabbit
melts, his fine blood-matted hair
dissolves to mold. The fertile year

revolves toward ground fog after rain,
and where the pheasants fed, raw blood-
root and skunk cabbage blur the line
of fenceposts. No distances define

what's near. Nor yet, in these rich signs
that blend toward spreading camouflage,
grows any sight of summer vines
that will choke the birch with lush designs.

PHILIP BOOTH *was born in New Hampshire in 1925. He currently lives in Lincoln, Mass., and is Assistant Professor of English at Wellesley. His long poem to Thoreau won the Hokin Prize in 1955 and his first book,* Letter from a Distant Land, *was awarded this year's Lamont Poetry Prize by the Academy of American Poets.*

Albatross

As his great wings the albatross
So delicately turns to subtle planes
And height won holds uncounted leagues across
The seas, through all that ever-changing air
Not motionless but almost so, so slow
Descending to Sun-varnished sea,
Rain-pebbled sea,
   soft misted sea;

As he those great,
   (by all accounts
Twelve feet or more),
   white wings outspreads
And, head bent down
For miles on end
Glides down this globe
   No home knowing, home-going though,
     —Home is with fellows
   For those great birds, in periodic turn,
   In sarabande, in formal round
     Oh those white birds,
   Moving solemn up and down
     Veering in their slow circle
   On the grey sea's heaving—

Death, Death, I go home
On solitary wings
And I go slow
No voice to sing,
No voice to tell what may be leagues,
To mark those grey untermined seas.

Two Garden Scenes

Horace, for whom I entertain
A high regard, inveighs against
One ingrate tree, which falling down,
Of its deceit near slew him, in the grounds
Of his own garden, when sitting quite unaware
Of any danger present there

Whatsoever; while Bishop Taylor tells us
How when that poet, Aeschylus,
Leaned back against his garden wall his baldpate shone
As if it were a great white stone;
Eagle dropped oyster to crack its shell
And pierced instead the poor man's skull.

Should it really surprise us though that the old man
(Death, I mean,) be so facetious? Surely no more than
This: that while so defying gravity (bone on dry bone
Balanced so delicately, no muscle binding—balance alone),
That while so tempting gravity
He maintain such tenacity;

For always is linked the unexpected
And those living and those dead
Are, by Death (that old schizo),
Neither more so nor less so
Linked, than Death himself
With everything else . . .

Five Serpents

Though I have not seen the milk snake
I have been told of his doings,
How that sly slithey, under night,
Entwines to rise, caduceus-like, the bovine thigh
To suck the creamy sweetness of her teats.

Of Eden I have read and further seen,
For all the world like some deceitful dictioner,
The great blue snake of Michigan, the racer,
Hang beckoning from his old tree
Beyond a sultry Sunday hill.

29

I have chattered walking pasturewise
As careless as a brittle bird,
Then frozen at the green grass-worm
That gartered from my thoughtless shoe
In rapid rabbit-innocence.

Yes—and in the rockbound pool below the falls
Have drifted lazy on my back,
Have slow-stroked calm in nakedness
Within the tree-encircled sky—then turned to see,
A reach away, the moccasin's drab eyes.

But once, as child and vaguely bound for school,
I peregrined to dawdle by a house exceeding strange;
I saw an arm, black-bombazined, slide through a half-closed
    door.
Upon my mind it coiled and struck;
A mark it left, intense and cold.

Lady and Crocodile

How calm and proud that lady, Nefertiti, walked
Beside her warm and black and ever-flowing Nile,
While lotus bloomed and small bird sang,
            while in her train the stalks
Of grey papyrus bent and fell, before one mournful croco-
    dile.

To heaven did the lady stand, robed all in night,
Yet she in loveliness outshone that star encrusted gown,
Her arm, her foot, her every part,
            in movement and in mold so right,
It bound the once in-finite space, made everlasting sound.

Now when this lady gazed on him he could not keep
Tear from his eye, so sad he was until she smiled
And spoke,
            "Upon such night it is not right that you should
                weep,
It is not right, Lord Crocodile, that you defile
            that so distinctly royal profile."

30

Just this she said, yet all the priests of Kom Ombus
        who crocodiles
Did feed, who scaly necks did hang with jewels,
        who prayers
Did say and litanies, did never please or so beguile
One crocodile, as did this slight cajolery
        of lady kindly fair.

Good madam, as you walk abroad upon such starry night,
Consider what poor crocodile may linger in your train
One moment turn, on him bestow, however slight,
A smile, a tender phrase,
        and then
(Though only if you feel you must)
        begin your walk again. . . .

CHARLES BURGESS, *born in New York City in 1924, is a graduate of Vanderbilt University, and has pursued advanced studies at Bread Loaf and at Columbia University. He has also been a traveling book peddler and a barker, sold time for a radio station, run an employment agency, and worked in a department store. At present he is a teacher at Kansas State Teachers College, in Pittsburg, Kans.*

JAN BURROWAY

Song

With whomsoever I share the spring
        I share my mouth,
    And credit to him all birth, all south,
        All seasoning,

Who flies with the first bland breath of May
        To my chill bed.
Then whatsoever the vows I've said
        And will yet say,

    There is no stirring of truth in me
        But to the season.
I tell you this that you may work treason
        On perjury,

And whomsoever you find untrue,
Imprison to spend all springs with you.

Owed to Dickens, 1956

A chef whose hat is celluloid and green,
Whose pots are paste-pots, and whose spice is spleen,
Has cooked my goose. And even now is wooding
The stove to offer up December pudding
So lumped and limp no Scrooge would dare dispatch it
Toward the Christmas feast of any Cratchit.
I can conjure visions of his doings:
Deadlines thudding due, and winter brewings
Steaming from the copy desk technician,
Even as I scan the May edition.
No Chuzzlewits, Pips, Pockets, Pumblechooks,
Invade his introverted pocketbooks,
But heroes grave, anemic and repressed,
And heroines perennially undressed;
Sex, sects and sin, seduction and sedition,
And prices slightly higher Denver west.

Oh, I'm a modern child. I'm overjoyed
With doses of cod liver oil and Freud.
But All The Year 'Round, modern publications
Grind to grounds my greatest expectations,
And psycho-pseudo-subtleties look quaint
By one brand of Victorian restraint;
Ah, label me a love-sick infidel,
But give me Tiny Tim and Little Nell,
A Magwitch and a Wopsle and a Wemmick,
And happy endings grandly epidemic.
Go feed your slice-of-life stuff to the chickens;
I'll be content when I'm full of the Dickens,
Where Fagins fail, and Dorrits get their due,
Where Olivers and Orlick *font la queue*
With Pickwicks clicking as the trick plot thickens,
And Dickens doling out the derring-do.

JAN BURROWAY *was born in Arizona in 1936 and is at present a senior at Barnard College in New York. Her poetry has appeared in* Seventeen *and* The Atlantic Monthly.

CONSTANCE CARRIER

Party

Eight years old, crouched in a corner, eyeing the others
  askance,
is King Arthur, or one of his knights, with helmet and shield
  and lance.

Stolid, his lip out-thrust, he is stubborn, he will not stir:
he fingers the plastic shield with its blazoned *Excalibur*.

Captain Video, stratosphere aces, jet pilots, men from Mars—
he watches them straddle the universe, their rocket guns
  shooting stars.

Full of tomorrow's world and the wars of tomorrow, they
  titter
or, worse, do not even look at Arthur, brooding and bitter.

Solicitude, bending to cheer him, is warned away by his
  face . . .
What is the archaic now, in a world all future and space?

Colonel B.

Eight lines of clergymen converged
to meet in Aaron Burr:
Edwardses, Tuthills, Pierreponts — each
a blood-and-thunderer
whose brimstone fire and sulphur smell
transfixed the listener.

Eight lines of clergymen converged,
as I have said, in Burr,
but Aaron was Beelzebub
in mocking miniature
who cast Religion forth and had
no further truck with her.

So oddly contradictory
the parts of Aaron were,

not all of us can damn him quite
without some faint demur —
rascal and profligate indeed,
scholar and sophister

(that fox's profile, sharp and small):
the suave practitioner
of his own ethic: Arnold's man,
a brilliant officer
("—untrustworthy," said Washington,
unable to concur):

a Catiline, to whom young men
would eagerly defer:
corrupter of the innocent:
condemned a murderer:
chevalier, if not *sans reproche*
past any doubt *sans peur:*

his daughter's idol, and his wife's:
almost an emperor:
a skyrocket for his device,
ambition for a spur:
"Too much Voltaire, too little Sterne":
both cynic and poseur,

witty, persuasive and urbane —
the pictures blend and blur . . .
At eighty, unregenerate,
he died in character:
"—God's pardon?" "On that subject I
am coy," said Aaron Burr.

CONSTANCE CARRIER *was born in New Britain, Conn. Her poems have appeared in* The Atlantic Monthly, Harper's Magazine, Poetry, The Nation, *and* The New Yorker. *A graduate of Smith College, Miss Carrier lives in New Britain, where she is a teacher of Latin in the Senior High School. In 1954, a collection of her poems,* The Middle Voice, *won the Lamont Award.*

THOMAS COLE

Praise to Light

Shutters unhinge the bat, and brazen sun
    Dazzles the sleepy head.
Wherefore all this giddy praise to light?
    Tell my household rise,
Throw off the night. Before the dew vapors
    From flower and roof, shake out
Those bitter dreams! What proof more the mind
    Be free? Freckled and fleet,
Accept the dare. Greet with an eye to love
    The hard or simple chore.

Old Woman's Song

"In youth I frowned
At dirt and broke
Brightest bloom
With pinch or poke,

"Dreamed of love
As gardened space
And hid in phlox
My anguished face.

"And then love came.
With but rude hands
He touched this body
Into radiance.

"Now crooked spine
Sustains the soul
And twisted fingers
Rout the mole.

"My back, my back!"
Old woman cries
Who grows the roses
Of Paradise.

36

By the Beautiful Sea

Lady, do not hold your parasol
To shun the sun. The tincture of your mole
Is proper proof, a little sun is all
You really need. Off with that winding stole!
There's more than time enough to mock the brown
With creams and lotions once you're back in town.

This sea resort is patterned on the bright
Idea summer is for your delight,
Thou widowed matron or thou bachelor girl.
Isn't this the beach where Mildred's curl
Was lost to Dawson? He used his picnic knife.
Later he sent salt kisses to his wife.

And sheltered groves are welcomes in disguise
For those who do not tend to be too wise.
Thus with your guile do not berate this place,
For though you dominate with subtle grace
That sandy bar intent on Nashe or Donne,
Remember your days are waning with the sun.

Display your wiles as you display your brain,
Take sloe gin straight, avoid the "bracing" tea.
Unbend your voice. Don't be a precious bane.
The soft pulsations of the swelling sea
Take for your very own. With errant sailors stray
Where you please. Lady, no parasol. Be gay!

THOMAS COLE *was born in 1922 in Baltimore, Md. Holder of degrees from Muhlenberg College and the University of Pennsylvania, Mr. Cole has published widely in this country and in magazines from Japan and India to London. His first volume of poems,* A World of Saints, *appeared in 1956. Editor of* Imagi, *Mr. Cole lives in Baltimore, where he teaches English.*

noone and a star stand,am to am

noone and a star stand,am to am

(life to life;breathing to breathing
flaming dream to dreaming flame)

united by perfect nothing:

millionary wherewhens distant,as
reckoned by the unimmortal mind,
these immeasurable mysteries
(human one;and one celestial)stand

soul to soul:freedom to freedom

till her utmost secrecies and his
(dreaming flame by flaming dream)
merge—at not imaginable which

instant born,a(who is neither each
both and)Self adventures deathlessness

maggie and milly and molly and may

maggie and milly and molly and may
went down to the beach(to play one day)

and maggie discovered a shell that sang
so sweetly she couldn't remember her troubles,and

milly befriended a stranded star
whose rays five languid fingers were;

and molly was chased by a horrible thing
which raced sideways while blowing bubbles:and

may came home with a smooth round stone
as small as a world and as large as alone.

For whatever we lose(like a you or a me)
it's always ourselves we find in the sea

i am a little church(no great cathedral)

i am a little church(no great cathedral)
far from the splendor and squalor of hurrying cities
—i do not worry if briefer days grow briefest,
i am not sorry when sun and rain make april

my life is the life of the reaper and the sower;
my prayers are prayers of earth's own clumsily striving
(finding and losing and laughing and crying)children
whose any sadness or joy is my grief or my gladness

around me surges a miracle of unceasing
birth and glory and death and resurrection:
over my sleeping self float flaming symbols
of hope,and i wake to a perfect patience of mountains

i am a little church(far from the frantic
world with its rapture and anguish)at peace with nature
—i do not worry if longer nights grow longest;
i am not sorry when silence becomes singing

winter by spring,i lift my diminutive spire to
merciful Him Whose only now is forever:
standing erect in the deathless truth of His presence
(welcoming humbly His light and proudly His darkness)

E. E. CUMMINGS *was born in Cambridge, Mass., in 1894 and received an M.A. from Harvard in 1916. After service in World War I, he wrote* The Enormous Room *(1922), now recognized as one of the great novels of that war. He has published numerous books of poetry and his collected poems were published in 1954. He is a member of the National Institute of Arts and Letters.*

BABETTE DEUTSCH

Earliness at the Cape

The color of silence is the oyster's color
Between the lustres of deep night and dawn.
Earth turns to absence; the sole shape's the sleeping
Light — a mollusk of mist. Remote,
A sandspit hinges the valves of that soft monster
Yawning at Portugal. Alone wakeful, lanterns
Over a dark hull to eastward mark
The tough long pull, hidden, the killing
Work, hidden, to feed a hidden world.
Muteness is all. Even the greed of the gulls
Annulled, the hush of color everywhere
The hush of motion. This is the neap of the blood,
Of memory, thought, desire; if pain visits
Such placelessness, it has phantom feet.
What's physical is lost here in ignorance
Of its own being. That solitary boat,
Out fishing, is a black stroke on vacancy.
Night, deaf and dumb as something from the deeps,
Having swallowed whole bright yesterday, replete
With radiance, is grey as abstinence now.
But in this nothingness, a knife-point: pleasure
Comes pricking; the hour's pallor, too, is bladed
Like a shell, and as it opens, cuts.

Morning Workout

The sky unfolding its blankets to free
The morning.
Chill on the air. Clean odor of stables.
The grandstand green as the turf,
The pavilion flaunting its brilliance
For no one.
Beyond hurdles and hedges, swans, circling, cast
A contemplative radiance over the willows' shadows.
Day pales the toteboard lights,
Gilds the balls, heightens the stripes of the poles.

40

Dirt shines. White glisten of rails.
The track is bright as brine.
Their motion a flowing,
From prick of the ear to thick tail's shimmering drift,
The horses file forth.
Pink nostrils quiver, as who know they are showing their
    colors.
Ankles lift, as who hear without listening.
The bay, the brown, the chestnut, the roan have loaned
Their grace to the riders who rise in the stirrups, or hunch
Over the withers, gentling with mumbled song.
A mare ambles past, liquid eye askance.
Three, then four, canter by: voluptuous power
Pours through their muscles,
Dancing in pulse and nerve.
They glide in the stretch as on skis.
Two
Are put to a drive:
Centaur energy bounding as the dirt shudders, flies
Under the wuthering pace,
Hushes the hooves' thunders,
The body's unsyllabled eloquence rapidly
Dying away.
Dark-skinned stable-boys, as proud as kin
Of their display of vivacity, elegance,
Walk the racers back.
Foam laces the girths, sweaty haunches glow.
Slowly returning from the track, the horse is
Animal paradigm of innocence, discipline, force.
Blanketed, they go in.
Odor of earth
Enriches azuring air.

BABETTE DEUTSCH (*Mrs. Avrahm Yarmolinsky*), *a native New Yorker, was born in 1895. Author of seven books of poetry, of which the latest is* Animal, Vegetable, Mineral, *she has also written works of criticism, one of which,* Poetry in our Time, *has just been reissued. Her most recent work is* Poetry Handbook: A Dictionary of Terms. *Miss Deutsch holds an honorary Litt. D. from Columbia University, where she lectures on Twentieth Century Poetry in English; she lives in New York City.*

The Rider

It is the East we dream of: there
We'd find the answer to despair,
The waters sweet, the women fair.

Seekers of truth ride through our land.
They scorn our commonplace and wend
Eastward. This we can understand.

There came a rider reined his beast
Beside our fountain, cried "At last
I've reached the waters of the East!"

The East our shabby countryside
And nothing more? "You lie!" we cried,
And so we stoned him till he died.

The Middle Ages: Two Views
I. Con

The wicked barons laid the landscape waste
With their two obsessions, hunting and battle.
They were always riding down something, man or beast,
And they placed the peasant on a par with cattle.

Castles were lordly prisons, ladies found life a bore
With their men forever away on feud or crusade.
They kept such open-house for the troubadour
That Holy Church anathemized his trade.

Their vices burned them spindleshanked and white,
(The tapestry-people prove this, says Michelet.)
Even crowned kings could seldom read or write
And villeins slept in sties and ploughed all day.

They had schools for magic, and the *droit du seigneur*,
And a low taste in fun, like the Feast of Fools.
There were racks, and covens of witches. They baited bears
And they had Gilles de Rais and plague and ducking-stools.

42

They ate with their fingers, and quite learned scholars
Debated how many angels could dance on a pin.
They thought the earth was flat, and serfs wore collars
Of iron, and every pleasure was a sin.

II. Pro

They enjoyed their times so much they pictured Paradise
As a little compact city with walls and spires,
With the Blesséd walking about in pointed shoes
And stylish liripipes among rose-thorn and pears.

They worshipped courtesy and chastity and courage
And Woman: there was always a knight on the road
Glittering off to rescue a lady. The woods' foliage
Rustled with fairy hinds and Robin Hood.

They liked the beasts: the pious, fantastic towers
Prickled with pointed stone ears. They were subtle in love,
Craft-proud, ardent. Saints sprang up like flowers,
And that life was often merry the *fabliaux* prove.

The lands glowed like a painted tabard with tourneys,
They had exquisite ivories, Dante and Joan of Arc.
They were always jogging about on exciting journeys
To Canterbury (see Chaucer), the Grail, or the Holy Rock,

And they lived cheek by jowl with surprise and miracle!
They believed in mermen and elves and the Judgement Horn;
The Queen of Heaven might appear at some holy well
And any thicket hide the unicorn.

LEAH BODINE DRAKE, *born in Chanute, Kans., in 1914, now lives
in Evansville, Ind. Her most recent volume of poems,* This Tilt-
ing Dust, *won the 1954 Borestone Mountain Award. She has
contributed poems to* The Saturday Review, The New Yorker,
The Atlantic Monthly, *and many other periodicals, and in June
of this year* The Atlantic Monthly *printed her essay on modern
poets.*

LORA DUNETZ

Black Cat

Black cat, black cat, with the lucky white spot at your neck,
In the angled shape of your face, in your eyes, there is Nile;
Your sacred ancestors have left their indelible mark.
Alley sprite, armchair pet, fond of a kitchen meal

Of fish, you have discerned the major purpose
Of our lives—to feed you, open doors,
To keep you warm, and unobtrusively to be of feline service.
Among the backyard weeds, no trespassers

Are safe, no bird to sing, nor dog explore.
—Black kittens fill your sheltered life by dozens,
Concealed from us, your servants, in our cellar,
Till step by cellar step, for private reasons

They seek the kitchen light. Those that survive
Their infancy, black cat, will make some man their slave.

The Ailing Parent

Pity this man who, slave to an affliction,
Enslaves his drifting world beyond love's premise,
Fastens a chain, ties a multiple noose;
No son escapes beyond his door.

                                He weaves
His self-destruction, not his self-protection,
For, crying
Each day: *My end!* each evening: *I am dying!*
He lives forever, while his children perish.

All That Summer

All that summer we pursued the butterflies,
Surrounding them in a maze of fingers. Ignorance wounded
The innocence that mantled our injury, and we mounted
The powdery creatures, golden wings full spread under glass,

Soft-bedded on white cotton. Thus suspended in perpetual
Semiflight, we assigned them to alien walls.
Strange how the passing of a little time reconciles
Us, alienates us from sin. Whole

Philosophies develop and shatter between
The child's mind and the adult's. We preserve,
Until we cease, the image that flits across the nerve
And lose, perhaps forever, the thing that we imprison

Into permanence. And still the winged things are not
Safe from capture; for whether we reach
Into space a practised hand and clasp them, or whether we
    clutch
Them from a trusted shoulder where they alight,

We doom their sanctuary. Out of the slime
Of eons they grew, for our Eden, ascended into
Our destruction, where childlike or childish we pursue
Them into worlds where mutual worlds are overcome.

LORA DUNETZ, *born in New York City, served during the Korean emergency as a First Lieutenant in the Women's Medical Specialist Corps. By profession an occupational therapist, she now lives in Baltimore, Md. Poems and reviews by Miss Dunetz have appeared in* Furioso, Imagi, Poetry, *and two* Epos *anthologies.*

RICHARD EBERHART

A Stone

A stone the size of man was my stone.
I did not throw it to the skies.
I did not kick it with my toe.
I held it in my hand, all alone.

And dreaming on the centuries,
This stone became a gentle dove
And dove-like flew upon the skies
In turns and ardors of fresh love.

It flew around a world of trust
In fine similitude. Its care
Astonished me, and loosed and lit
The eyes of lovers everywhere.

In the Garden

Memory is a watery flower, when watered
Will transplant a scent from A to Z;
It is September. There are zephyrs truly.
A gold-banded bee in russet loam

Throws off the earth, his heavy cargo
At last aloft. You are the medium.
In you the subtle messages suspend
The alphabeta particles of gauze

Realization claiming permanence.
For these zephyrs, these sights and sounds,
That heavy bee, those indeterminate scents
Are not the world, but they are you.

You know them sitting in the shade
In old September, by the rich red banks.
The zephyrs are your mind, a probable
Stored world of melos appetite.

The Lost Children

And so the river moves,
Impersonal and slow
Today. Let us go,
Afraid to own our loves,

To the place of ice and snow,
The brink where yesterday
Two children, held aglow,
Walked time away.

In a moment they were lost.
Ignorance and innocence
Pulled them under and tossed
Their souls up from sense.

Now, O stars, you hold
Their small souls, two
Children cold and old
In lissome Spring the true.

And so the river moves
Impersonal and slow.
We watch. Let us go,
And hold close our loves.

RICHARD EBERHART, *born in Austin, Minn., in 1904, was educated at Dartmouth, Cambridge University, and Harvard. His recent books include* Selected Poems, *1951;* Undercliff, *1953; and* Great Praises, *which appeared this year. He has won the Shelley Memorial Prize, the Harriet Monroe Poetry Award from the University of Chicago, and a National Institute Award. Given an honorary Litt. D. by Dartmouth in 1954, he is now Poet in Residence and Professor of English at Dartmouth.*

ANNEMARIE EWING

The Man Within

Mesdames, never dare to deem those lovers yours
Who only squire you, house you, husband you;
Very well. Be squired, be housed, be married, too;
But never dare to deem those lovers yours.

Hie you to party and game with them, hie you to bed.
Hie you to supermarket, with bassinet;
Lovely the strains of the he-and-she minuet —
Be partnered, mesdames, but never be misled.

All of your squires and husbands, love them well.
They are all Nature's necessary men,
Not yours, mesdames. Look kindly on them, then,
And with them learn, in amity, to dwell.

But do not confuse any one of them with him
Who waits for you to light, though he forbid,
The candle that reveals him, as Psyche did.
Thereafter he may, winged like seraphim,

Waft you to virtue; or, demon-like, drown you in sin
Until you acknowledge his presence as one that endures,
The only lover who is eternally yours,
Your other half, mesdames, the man within.

Fisherman's Blunder Off New Bedford, Massachusetts

You — Mermaid! Your sea-green hair and sin-sweet singing
Bewitch me. Come aboard! (Strong snood for her hair, he
    thought;
Homespun for her shameless nakedness; and, for her singing,
More seemly music. A lass must be properly taught.)
His outstretched hands, like hers, were wet and clinging;
She rose to the bait of his sea-salt lips — and was caught.

48

Home sailed the fisherman then, exultant to beach her.
(*Now* we'll have music, he thought, with this tamed pretty
    thing
Demure by my hearth where no sea-got tunes can reach her;
Anthem and lullaby all her caroling.)
Pity that every song he tried to teach her
Made it more difficult for her to sing.

If the Heart Be Homeless

What is this whisper of homelessness, good my heart,
Sudden a sullen stranger in my breast?
Sudden these flickering visions and dreams invade me;
At your behest?

Are there not good things at hand here: love? and art?
And work? familiar means to desirable ends;
Are there not shelter and food and the good Lord who made
    me?
Are there not friends?

What distant demesne have you dwelt in, good my heart,
Whose mountains are native to you and whose songs are
    your songs?
How slowly I learn that a heart loses homelessness only
Where it belongs;

How tardily turn to your compass and sextant and chart. . . .
God help me through what flood or fire the journey may lie!
But we're long overdue at your home, poor exiled and lonely,
And wiser than I.

ANNEMARIE EWING (*Mrs. John H. Towner*) *was born in Pittsburgh, Pa., in 1910. She is the author of a novel,* Little Gate, *and of short stories published in* The Ladies' Home Journal, Seventeen, *and* The Saturday Evening Post, *and has contributed articles to* The New Yorker, Downbeat, *and* Radio Mirror. *Miss Ewing now lives in Los Angeles, Calif., where she works for the Board of Education.*

THOMAS HORNSBY FERRIL

Kochia

Undulations of precision harass the mind,
We claim by forgery the signatures of wind.

When I was a child I plunged headlong into the weeds,
Good hiding in a game the moonlight counted out,
Still as a fawn I lay, the tang of the pursuers
Treading the greenness of my eager nostrils.

Later I learned the names of these tall weeds
That sheltered me.
The names are imprecise,
They are not wonder.

What Trinkets?

The candle-blossoms of horse-chestnut left
Me seven leaves that pronged from a single stem
The last day of October. I could feel
The blueness through them and all being through them.

It was as if some funeral procession
Had wandered through some pom-pom-pullaway town
Where children pranced and skulls recalled no lips
They'd worn to feel the press of kisses on.

What trinkets are impedible to vision?
I know of none: the harbors float at will
Across my mountains and all generations
Flicker in the embers on the hill.

The Man Who Thought He Was a Horse

There was a man in Denver
Who thought he was a horse,
I'll show you where he lived and where he died,
The man could pull a buggy
And the man could pull a hearse
But he couldn't get up on his back and ride.

It started when he'd whinny
As a boy down in the pasture,
Each morning he would race the morning train,
The fireman clanged and whistled
To make him gallop faster,
Then he'd prance and curry cinders from his mane.

He licked a salty mountain
And he struck a lode of gold
That paid him weekly fifty thousand dollars,
He built a great big castle
And he decked the castle walls
With whiffletrees and jeweled hames and collars.

He kept a hundred mares
And he owned four daily papers,
He was kind to the poor and he wined the presidents,
But he hid in the dark
When the circus came to town,
He was leery of the droppings of the elephants.

He'd hang around the fire house
To watch them train the horses,
They'd canter down the street in teams of three,
He'd pace them on the sidewalk
With blinders on his eyes,
His knee action was wonderful to see.

He was very very strong
And very very gentle,
He'd piss on the fireworks at the country club,
He'd roll on his back
In bank directors' meetings,
He was sociable and difficult to snub.

He shied one day
At a one-lung car
While speaking at a statue of a stud,
He ran away and died
On an iron picket fence,
And a patch of oats grew up out of his blood.

Basic Communication

Such dubious nomenclatures crowding in
Around, above, below direct intent:
You said I said you said I said begin
Again with what I meant you meant I meant.

We speak by musclings of after-rote,
The lust in us deserves and earns the quarrel,
The waggle tongue is captain of the throat,
No victory, no grace, no sprig of laurel.

THOMAS HORNSBY FERRIL *was born in Denver, Colo., in 1896. He still makes his home there, and is employed by the Great Western Sugar Company as an expert in educational work in agriculture. He has published four books of poetry, the latest being* New and Selected Poems, *as well as a book of prose essays,* I Hate Thursday. *His awards include prizes from* The Nation, Poetry, The Academy of American Poets, *and* The Forum, *and he has received honorary degrees from Colorado College, Colorado University, and the University of Denver. With his wife, Helen R. Ferril, he edits the inimitable weekly,* The Rocky Mountain Herald, *founded in 1860, "the oldest weekly newspaper in Colorado."*

DAVID FERRY

The Unawkward Singers

Self-praise is a wonderful thing!
It causes all the birds to sing:
The sparrow's brag, thrush's conceit,
They make the whole world cheerly repeat
Cheerly repeat their praise.

For any lark there is no other,
No father, mother, sister, brother,
No sweet wife, nor no dear love;
The dove's the pool in which the dove,
Loving, admires his ways.

Wind out of the swan's throat
His final, operatic note:
Impassioned on himself he dies,
Knowing the world is him, is his
By his self-celebration.

Master man cannot so please
Himself with eloquence like these;
Thus clumsily his song is sung,
Thick praise by a thick tongue
For its own limitation.

Poem About Waking

I knew once,
In your embrace,
The need that thence
I soon must pass,
And find my age
Some other place,
And thus in rage
I loved, alas!

The Antagonist

I saw a man come down to the furious sea.
He had a beard, and in that beard were birds.
He stood between the sea and a green tree
And brushed those birds away. They flew like words
Out of his crystal beard, they flew away,
Skittering into the sky, and soon were gone.
This was a man who had a crystal eye,
And all turned crystal that he looked upon.
Divinity flowers here, he said, and here
Also. And in the wind. How crystal-clear
Divinity blooms, in sea, and wind, and wood.
It is like light, and light like God, and good.

Then sure enough the world was all one flower
Of crystal light, and lost in the light was I,
Was the tree, were the birds, and the fish in his power
Were lost in the light-lost sea, till stubbornly I
Stood still in that light, and tore and tore with my tongue
At that prisoning flower, imagining till all the birds
Sang loud again in that wood, till again the fish sang
In the furious sea, echoing my fierce words,
Fantastic birds roaring in *that* green wood!
I would not give assent to what he said.
I stood in that place till crystal lay all about me.
Imagine your heaven, I cried, but do it without me!

Out of That Sea

As shepherd and shepherdess, how many summers had we
Sung mourning and praising? Our sheep were lulling and
    drowsing;
Like bottomless pools our cattle lay lolling long.
Love, said our pipes, love, love, cried the cattle bird skim-
    ming
The piebald depths of those cows. All afternoon drifted;
And dreaming we lay as the light and the sea-shade shifted.

It was then that we drowned in the sleep and deep dream of
    that beauty,

54

Thanking our deaths as we turned, slowly and slowly,
Falling through light we fell to the golden floor.
We alighted like angels, and all in our dreaming we danced,
Fantastic, slow, wonderful turning and courtesy.
The sea-caves rang with the wonder, fish sang for the beauty!

Then together we rose, and together and hand in hand,
We went through a landscape neither ideal nor pretty,
Coming to ruin. Nearby, in a hickory tree,
The wise old owl sat mute. From his eye a glare
Shone loud and clear in the calm evening air.
From the hoot of that eye we shrank in our sudden fear,

And together, I turning to you, you turning to me,
We saw how our hands came wrinkled out of that sea.

On the Way to the Island

After we fled away from the shuddering dock,
The sea upheld us, would not let us go
Nor drown us, and we danced all night in the dark,
Till we woke to discover the deck was made of glass,
All glass, and, leaning together, we lovers looked down,
Say a hundred miles, say a million years, and there
Were the fish, huge, munching, graceless, flashing
Their innocent frightening scales in the dark!

My lady wears brilliants in her hair, and the sun
Makes their fakery sparkle, so beautiful
Is she my lady, so pitiful is she,
Her white arms so naked after those scales,
Her coquetry pretty after those monsters
Beginning her history there in the deep dark.
My lady, I love you because of the dark
Over which your glass slippers so ignorantly danced!

DAVID FERRY, *born in Orange, N. J., in 1924, is Assistant Pro-fessor of English at Wellesley College. His poems have appeared in* The New Yorker, The Kenyon Review, *and* The Paris Re-view, *among other places, and he was also represented in* Best Poems of 1955, *which received a Borestone Mountain Poetry Award.*

ROBERT FRANCIS

The Seed-Eaters

The seed-eaters, the vegetarian birds,
Redpolls, grosbeaks, crossbills, finches, siskins,
Fly south to winter in our north, so making
A sort of Florida of our best blizzards.

Weed seeds and seeds of pine cones are their pillage,
Alder and birch catkins, such vegetable
Odds and ends as the winged keys of maple
As well as roadside sumac, red-plush-seeded.

Hi! with a bounce in snowflake flocks come juncos
As if a hand had flipped them and tree sparrows,
Now nip and tuck and playing tag, now squatting
All weather-proofed and feather-fluffed on snow.

Hard fare, full feast, I'll say, deep cold, high spirits.
Here's Christmas to Candlemas on a bunting's budget.
From this old seed-eater with his beans, his soybeans,
Cracked corn, cracked wheat, peanuts and split peas, hail!

Cold

Cold and the colors of cold: mineral, shell,
And burning blue. The sky is on fire with blue
And wind keeps ringing, ringing the fire bell.

I am caught up into a chill as high
As creaking glaciers and powder-plumed peaks
And the absolutes of interstellar sky.

Abstract, impersonal, metaphysical, pure,
This dazzling art derides me. How should warm breath
Dare to exist? Exist, exult, endure?

Hums in my ear the old Ur-father of freeze
And burn, that pre-post-Christian Fellow before
And after all myths and demonologies.

Under the glaring and sardonic sun,
Behind the icicles and double glass
I huddle, hoard, hold out, hold on, hold on.

Boy Riding Forward Backward

Presto, pronto! Two boys, two horses.
But the boy on backward riding forward
Is the boy to watch.

He rides the forward horse and laughs
In the face of the forward boy on the backward
Horse, and *he* laughs

Back and the horses laugh. They gallop.
The trick is the cool barefaced pretense
There is no trick.

They might be flying, face to face,
On a fast train. They might be whitecaps
Hot-cool-headed,

One curling backward, one curving forward,
Racing a rivalry of waves.
They might, they might—

Across a blue of lake, through trees,
And half a mile away I caught them:
Two boys, two horses.

Through trees and through binoculars
Sweeping for birds. Oh, they were birds
All right, all right,

Swallows that weave and wave and sweep
And skim and swoop and skitter until
The last trees take them.

ROBERT FRANCIS, *born in Upland, Pa., in 1901, has lived most of his life in Amherst, Mass. Author of four volumes of poems and a short novel, he does summer teaching and lecturing at Chautauqua, N. Y., and for 1957-58 holds an Academy in Rome Fellowship from the American Academy of Arts and Letters.*

On Reading the Metamorphoses

Gods and furies now depart.
Myth again inhabits dust;
sweating flesh, divided, must
resume the burden of the heart.

Hunter and the hunted are
emblems of the same desire.
Inner image and the star
burn alive with the same fire.

Those whom suffering forgives,
that which brutally is torn
to pieces, are reborn.
"Then chiefly lives."

Caedmon

All uncompelled, weightless as the notes
wrung out of bells at kindling dawn,
more light-thrilled than a shallow stream
over brute rock dashed, these thoughts
flash to song like figures from a dream.

Creation roars. Happens in fire and flood
the riot which is God. A flock of hurts
(the sad crowd, grazing of bitter hearts,
the blank gaze, fright in the rotten wood)
released, reprieved, departs,

as, naked, empty as a broken bowl
of everything save light and air, I learn
to praise the water, praise the fire. Burns
then, eternal phoenix, all the soul
I was and I rejoice to be reborn.

Tiresias

Speak to us who
are also split.
Speak to the two
we love and hate.

You have been both
and you have known
the double truth
as, chaste, obscene,

you were the lover
and the loved.
You were the giver
who received.

Now tell us how
we can be one
another too.
Speak to us who

in single wrath
cannot be true
to life or death.
Blinder than you.

Snapshot: Politician

When I was at the funeral
he was more solemn and tiptoeing
than even the undertaker.
    For Christ's sake!

He had a big hand and a good word
for everybody. He was driving
an air-conditioned Cadillac.

His hair was black, luxuriant and curly as the
        wool on a ram;
and when he *did* smile it was like all the lights of
    a Christmas tree going on at once.

At the grave after the casket was lowered
(it went down so quickly, quietly it was astonishing)
somebody asked him about a speeding ticket.

"My word's good as far as the Savannah River,"
he said. "After that you're in the hands
    of Herman Talmadge."

Snapshot: Ambassadress

We had a parade for the lady near Livorno.
I spent a solid hour shining up my boots.

We got there and lined up,
        eight thousand men,
and waited quite a while because she was late.

Finally she showed up and drove up and down
trooping the line in a white jeep.
She said America would be proud of us
and what an important job we'd done in Trieste.

After it was all over and we were back in the tents,
a man in my squad (he was from Alabama) asked me:
"Say, Sarge, who the hell *was* that Clara Bell Lou
    we fell out for?"

Snapshot of a Pedant

Privately, your pencil makes
wry marginalia, doodles at the edge
of noted pages, underlines examples of
what you call the worst excesses.

"Puddles of Sentiment!" You scrawl
an epitaph for Shelley and his critics,
uneasy among the vague Romantics.

"Pope & Swift would have admired
        Bentley & Dennis
if only they had understood."
Thus gladly reconcile and make a peace
among the factions of your favorite century.

If I hide my mouth to laugh,
if I yawn, doze while you drone,
if, choking with frustration,
I curse you in the language of those years

for "a Blockhead and a fine dull Ass,"
I must (in truth) confess

your strictness is like a conscience,
your rigor's like the pattern which
the feet must follow in numbered silence
before they waltz free to real music.

One learns to count before one learns the dance.
One learns to speak grammatically before
one takes the stance of satire and/or praise.

And I have seen the virtue of
your passion for precision.
You teach, by vehement revision,
that labor is a way to love.

GEORGE GARRETT, *born in Orlando, Fla., in 1929, was a student at Princeton on the G.I. Bill after duty overseas in Austria and Germany as an enlisted man in the Field Artillery. His poems,* The Reverend Ghost, *appear this year in the* Poets of Today *series. Mr. Garrett has published half a dozen short stories, and is now teaching at Wesleyan University in Middletown, Conn. He won the Glascock Poetry Award in the 1952 competition at Mt. Holyoke College.*

WALKER GIBSON

The Game

October! Can I stand it one more year?
This Saturday they're playing at the Bowl!
Connecticut's afire with autumn cheer—
There's yellow-red nostalgia in my soul.
Rev up the old convertible, for I'm
Off to New Haven for the thousandth time.

Over and under parkway bridges gliding,
With Thunderbirds and Caddies flitting by,
Again October finds me riding, riding
Into that old familiar autumn sky
Through traffic gay with girls and garish grads,
Blankets, banners, chrysanthemums, and plaids.

Light lunch on someone's lawn—"Park right in here!"—
Ham or egg salad from a plastic basket
(Hammacher-Schlemmer: used it last last year),
Plus little swallows from a pocket flasket
To harden one to hail old friends by name—
"Say Mike!" "Say Mort!" "Say . . . ?" On, on! The Game!

Sluicing through Portal Twelve at two o'clock
(A to the right, B left, C straight ahead),
We reach a roost and perch among that flock,
Each with a pretty feather in its head.
Far far below on geometric green
Infinitesimal figures can be seen

Running and falling, falling and running, falling,
As in some ritual of holy dance.
With complicated forms of mauling sprawling,
The young rejuvenate arcane romance,
Chasing an egg (the rites of procreation),
Bowed down in mysteries of T-formation.

And every year I manage to forget
How absolutely dull the thing is, too.
That thumping music!—there's that old regret

These fifty thousands number me and you.
But now the first chill of late afternoon
Blows through the Bowl. It will be over soon.

Over and under parkway bridges gliding,
The Thunderbirds and Caddies flitting past,
October night will find us riding, riding
Back to the life we left behind at last.
Every autumn, autumn's a little colder.
Oh every fall I feel a full year older!

Love

How wasteful, as they say, is Nature.
Suckers spring from an old fruit tree
As if their green leaves had a future.
I know how it will be with me,
Some day, sidling along the street
(Through with that sort of thing forever),
Catching sight of an upturned throat,
Torn again with that old-fool fervor.

Advice to Travelers

A burro once, sent by express,
His shipping ticket on his bridle,
Ate up his name and his address,
And in some warehouse, standing idle,
He waited till he like to died.
The moral hardly needs the showing:
Don't keep things locked up deep inside—
Say who you are and where you're going.

WALKER GIBSON *was born in 1919, brought up in Albany, N. Y.,
and graduated from Yale. After four years in the Army Air
Forces, he served for a year as assistant in the Writers' Work-
shop at the University, and then joined the English Department
at Amherst College. His first book of poems,* The Reckless
Spenders, *was published in 1954. Mr. Gibson has recently been
appointed to the faculty of New York University.*

RICHARD GILLMAN

Snow Fell with a Will

Snow fell with a will as pure as snow,
Fell like some planet a last time stirred
Mysteriously crumbled and powdered
With a wind and with no word.

Skin felt its quick unfreezing, windfalls from
The place it froze, chimneys and chimneys away,
Up where cold airplanes belly-drop and sway,
Where human wishes, when they go, stay.

Fast down like only fear could draw it
If our world tonight were ending,
It blanketed too soberly, unbending,
As if our world tonight were ending.

Underfoot and overhead, over, under beauty,
Caught by the wind and pulling down the wind,
Unlining everything eyes had outlined,
It swirled to haze the most well-ordered mind.

God, if He were up there and not down,
And if He were only a force without our care
In view, would still have been especially aware
Of His angels flying bare.

Everything went under or came down.
Everything was surely out or in.
And mind, that had to let the stuff pour in,
Snuggled up to heart without a mention.

Snow fell with a light as sunless as dark,
Dark as non-human or inhuman business.
Nothing ours or what made earth seem ours to bless
Ever seemed ours less.

Moved by Her Music

Her loveliness stirred my circumstances
To new places and new poses,
Much as music moves the seated dancers.

But woman, it is maybe not so queer,
Can do that: can take a place
Ascending a mind, descending a stair,

Most forthright in her sole direction,
But helpless in her slow expression,
Touched with a rose of thornless fiction,

Moving in with such a nature,
Such sweeping, strange familiarity,
One is taken to possess her.

In Renoir's *Ball at Bougival*, she
Scarcely holds him, almost holds away,
But he is held completely,

Moved by her music, while really hearing none,
Intently, silently involved in being all
Of her earth-altering ambition.

RICHARD GILLMAN, *born in Northampton, Mass., in 1929, was stationed in the Canal Zone when he contributed to the first* New Poems. *A former newspaperman, he now works for a publishing house in New York City and makes his home in The Bronx.*

DONALD HALL

Five Epigrams

1. Begin again. There is no law which says
   That men must imitate their images.

2. Oh, happiness! he said, and took his life,
   But first, to make a marriage, shot his wife.

3. If *Self-regard* has golden wit,
   I'll pray that mine be counterfeit.
   It is by skill of artifice
   The alchemist makes that seem this.
   Without his skill, mere gold is dull,
   And with it, lead is beautiful.

4. Black is no color; white is all of sense.
       Yet in the choices of their acts, men live
   By the dark colors of experience;
       White purity is only negative.

5. "Mirror, mirror, on the wall,
       Who is Donald Andrew Hall?"
   "Self-knowledge is a rare disease.
       These words, Donald, are vanity's."

The Morning Porches

Even the morning is formal. A coughing dog
    scatters the birds, whose quick hysteria
Becomes a lady's fan against the fog.

I sit upon a changing porch, and think
    ideas about the insubstantial wood,
That I may make real porches out of ink.

This is a crazy morning. There are times
    when it seems highly serious to catch
The indeterminate between two rhymes.

Yet such a catch is fond, for in the act

analogy becomes the thing itself;
    Porches are made of wood; this is a fact.

So look again, and deeper. I have heard
    that though the animal is singular,
Two billion particles make up a bird.

Laocoon

I lived to tell the truth, and truth was wrong.
I threw the spear to save the multitude
Whose priest I was, and when the Trojan throng

Heard the long scream of pain, their changing mood
Turned awful welcome into sacrifice.
"Hurry!" I told them. "Give the fire its food!"

But truth in politics will not suffice.
(Troy was a hecatomb Ulysses made.)
The Gods who knew what armed, Ithacan mice

Hid in that hole, waiting the time to raid,
Sent house-high serpents hissing from the sea,
Whose apparition made all Troy afraid,

Who bound their coils around my sons and me
And rendered us to Hades in a piece.
The Gods who blessed the Greeks blessed perjury,

And smothered truth to win a war for Greece.

The Beautiful Horses

That time we went to Suffolk Downs to see
The flattened gallop of the thoroughbred,
The Morning Telegraph was what I had
To help me bet, on past and pedigree.

But you declared that racing forms were rot.
Before each race, rapt at the paddock rail,
You valued every horse from nose to tail,
And bet upon the pleasure that you got.

Although our ways of betting differed greatly,
Our wins and losses showed a strange conformance.

67

Maybe I knew, reading each Past Performance,
The quality you praised when they were stately.

Still, it was I who changed. That day, like Moses,
You led me to a place where I have settled,
Where horses graze on clover thickly petalled,
Beautiful winners, collared with pink roses.

for R. W.

DONALD HALL, *born in Connecticut in 1928, has been a Junior Fellow in the Society of Fellows at Harvard, and is now an Assistant Professor of English at the University of Michigan. His first book of verse,* Exiles and Marriages, *won the Lamont Award in 1955.*

JOHN HAY

Aboriginal Sin

I know derisive men and women,
I know myself. The deep derisions
Don't pray out. I hear a flicker call:
"Yackety-yak," and rat-a-hammer
Bore the dead oak for a fall.
Original sin is a misnomer.
It is aboriginal—the dove
An ancient turtle egging love.

Bird Song

Here! No sweetness trips so well as here,
Daylight! Daylight! lifting by.
Stray in the scatter of . . . do flowers say?
Where will you be off to, lovely, lovely?
No matter where? That's right. That's right.
The air! and careless, far, far . . . fly it. Fly

The Chickadees

First station off on a cold road to the country,
and a man stepped down into oblivion.
An uttermost, most plain and slate-eyed sky
said: "Back." It was coming on to snow.
This was dead end weather.
No one had told him in the nation
that it had a wilderness.
He looked around, with no way out.
Then something fluttered at a sign post
to give him new directions—
sky tops crossed with snow flakes, trees with birds
wild simmerings of company,
like black and white snow bursts tripped from dark twigs;
chips, cries, small hearts drumming with a fear
that must be joy, or why, despite himself
should he look up and laugh?

"The Energy of Light"

Hard on a high flower comes the sun;
It bullies the seed, and hurries on
The spider's blistering trapeze—
A highway, like our own spinning
Wild over age. It stops me nodding,
This send and spend by light—of lees,
Waste, or aggrandizement—put to us:
Love and learn, sink or swim, go to it,
Lest you never come to burn. Burning
Is an art, as much as flying is dying.
The nestling fear shoves off—will it fall?
It swoops, and fires the sky wall.

Old Man of Tennessee

He's slight and old and sits up timidly
Riding the bus in his own Tennessee,
Out of the mountain gaps that flow with stones
Where high fall's pitching, pillaging red leaves
Distance again the pioneer remains:
His own, back wooly fields and salient corn—
An old tobacco juicer who can't see
With pink-rimmed eyes what the world tries to be
Or where it goes. He is from under stars
And ricks and ribs unknown. His dry dog's beard
Dusts 'round Abe Lincoln's great broad monkey ears.
He has a neck as dark as coffee grounds
And history's nose, hawk-boned and mummified.
"Here, Uncle," the driver opens up the door
Next to a mountain and a sycamore.
Now the old man is back to where he was
And is and will be, shuffling off, left by,
No more than can be, and Thy Will Be Done.

JOHN HAY, *born in Ipswitch, Mass., in 1915, edited the army* weekly, Yank, *and has published one book of poems,* A Private History. *He is currently President of the Cape Cod Junior Museum, a natural-history museum for children, and is next fall publishing a book entitled* The Run, *a naturalist's account of the migration of the alewives, a species of herring.*

70

JAMES HAYFORD

Overseer of the Poor

The poor men's God that gives them sleep
Is not to be reproached because
By some the gift is reckoned cheap.

Let them sleep soundly on their straws
While rich men count expensive sheep.
God of the rich there never was.

In a Closed Universe

Children and pets, please note:
When one is pleased to dote,
Your part is to be grateful;
When you presume to expect
Indulgence, you seem hateful
And may be sharply checked.

That any live possession
Will thus commit aggression
Does seem unfortunate,
But in a closed universe
Love is the source of hate,
And favor is a curse.

See that you stand in awe
From childhood of this law
To ward off desperation
And heal the cruel cut
Whenever god or nation
Moodily says Tut tut.

Horn

O come sweet death, sang Bach,
Not instancing his own,
The man from Eisenach
Who kept the night alone,

Busy as it grew late
To wake the patient morn
With his own intricate
Simplicities of horn.

The Resident Worm

The pitcher plant makes a living by
Enticing living things to die
In quest of ruinous delight.
It keeps an apprentice that matures
On the rich harvest of its lures—
A resident worm or parasite.

On the other hand, the goldenrod
Survives invasion by a worm
That dines upon its endoderm
And winters in a private pod—
An ugly but benignant cyst
That isolates the colonist.

So life is given and taken in ways
That are too hard for us to praise—
Inhuman are the ways of God.

Under All This Slate

The bulletin of the boarding school—
Seventy lads, eleven masters—
Depicts the windowed swimming pool,
Autumnal pathways edged in asters,
Stout Georgian fronts with wide pilasters.

The Headmaster is Ph.D.
(Columbia), Princeton handles French,
English has published poetry,
The Board is winnowed from the bench,
Bar, bank, and International Wrench.

Sirs, somewhere under all this slate
You lodge, I see, a lad named Feeters.
Tell us the way he bears his fate.
Not mentioned in your prize competers,
Is he among your hearty eaters?

JAMES HAYFORD, *born in Montpelier, Vt., in 1913, has been Robert Frost Fellow of Amherst College, and has published poems in* Harper's Magazine, The New Yorker, *and* The Saturday Evening Post. *He is school music supervisor of the district around Orleans, Vt.*

JOHN HOLMES

The Chance

Chin in, I doubt the praying mantis prays.
His is an equally appropriate stance
For covering the back of his neck, or eyes,
Or for looking accidental to avoid accidents.

His name is one of those tedious unkillable
Incorrectnesses (ah, how significant
That even in this the gesture is possible)
We could rid our thinking of, and don't.

Enough (it's too much) that mantis means prophet,
Without cocking his elbows and wrists too.
Likelier it's for combat and discomfit,
Or all he knows really well how to do.

Still, there he was on the mailbox praying,
When I stopped to drop three important letters in,
Seeming to say about them what I was saying,
And wildly improbable, in my town.

No, life is sufficiently apparently absurd
To include this several-million-to-one chance.
It happens. It happened. One is not bored
In a world where everything happens at least once.

Carry Me Back

The big blue-jean, the summer-bored boy next door,
Has been marching through Georgia all afternoon.
Tramp, tramp, tramp on the piano, his fists have trod
The vineyard where my grapes of wrath are stored.
He has brought Johnny marching home again, again,
And tented on the old camp ground tonight once more.
I am a captive audience, neighbor slave to noise.

One-fingered, he wanders way down the Suwanee River,
Where his heart, like mine, that's where it's turning

Ever. He asks the key of F, C, or G to carry him back.
Carry me back to ole Virginny (now it's both hands)
Where the corn and taters grow, beyond this hot
Suburban house, family, no school, no job, no fun.

Back to where I used to banjo my way back to,
Andersonville, Gettysburg, the decks of the *Monitor*.
Gone are the days, but we hear the voices calling.

By way of Brady's camera, when I was this boy's age,
I wanted to creep near Lincoln and that chin-beard,
Through my uncle's stereopticon to Grant's staff tent,
And hear that posed group break it up, and talk,
Lincoln to Brady, Grant to Lincoln, the wrinkled generals,
Belted and bewhiskered, to one another and the dog.

I'd be there in a forage-cap, with a long bayonet
Fixed to my long rifle, and my own cartridge-belt.
I'd stand guard, a sentry, in the timbered trenches,
Those snug play-places in a home-war that made sad songs.
Old Black Joe. Old Abe Lincoln. Old Virginny.
Old camp ground. Old boy next door, and old me.

The Fortune Teller

At a university women's sort of charity fair,
With book-tables, and candy and greeting cards,
Where nobody knew me, and what I was doing there
I can't think now, a woman with fortune cards

Told fortunes. Who doesn't like it? I always do.
I crossed her palm with fifty cents, for the fund
For daughters of missionaries to Tierra del Fuego.
She decoded the cards, she read lines in my hand,

And said, "I see great happiness for you soon.
I see your life," she said, "moving in love
Among many who love you. What you fear is gone.
I see rewards you do not know you deserve.

You write. You will write beyond your secret hope.
You have children. All will be well with them,"
She said. I gave her money again. "Stop! Stop!"
I said. "Tell me the terrible truth of my palm,

75

The furrows of grief, the clatter of calamity,
Time's roof crashing, my very home my doom,
My poison myself." The woman looked at me,
Costumed, but my kind, our speech the same,

Was not a gypsy, of course, some college man's wife
Like my wife, telling fortunes, a stranger, too.
"Tell me," I said, "that nothing I do is safe,
That I must fail, must be destroyed, must die

In darkness crying out Mother, and die unheard.
Tell me the worst after worst, what will be taken
From me, and what taken after that, what feared
The most, and found out, and I on that broken."

She said, "Nothing will be taken. You walk in light.
Your cry is heard. Your mornings remember yesterdays
Of peace, and close with you come, early and late,
Of the unseparated in your love, these, these."

Who was she, nobody, everyone, so sure about this?
Fortune, a mirror, your own hand, yourself, she said.
But I was saying it, it was in my mouth a noise
As if I had been dead, and now was not dead.

JOHN HOLMES, *born in Somerville, Mass., in 1904, has been
editor, lecturer, and anthologist as well as teacher and poet.
Phi Beta Kappa Poet at Harvard in 1956, Mr. Holmes is Asso-
ciate Professor of English at Tufts University, and lives in Med-
ford, Mass. The latest of several books of poetry is* The Symbols.

BARBARA HOWES

The Triumph of Death

Illusion forms before us like a grove
Of aspen hazing all the summer air
As we approach a new plateau of love.

With discs of light and shade, vibration of
Leaf-candelabra, dim, all-tremulous there,
Illusion forms before us like a grove

And bends in welcome: with each step we move
Nearer, quick with desire, quick to dare.
As we approach a new plateau of love,

New passion, new adventure wait above
And call to our drumming blood; all unaware
Illusion forms before us like a grove

In a mirage, we reach out to take Love
In our arms, compelled by one another's stare.
As we approach a new plateau of love

The aspen sigh in mockery: then have
We come this way before? Staining the air,
Illusion forms before us like a grove
As we approach a new plateau of love.

The Triumph of Chastity

Over the plain two dark
Equestrian figures pound
Charging full tilt at spring;
Behind them burnt-over ground,
A desolate panel stretches,
A long dun scarf unwound.

The taller, Cavalier
Hatred, his horny gut
Wild with the heat of their ride
Spurs onward, faster yet
Must he race his mighty Arab
Stallion; upon her jennet

77

Side-saddle, stride for stride,
Gallops the Lady, fleet
Ambition; her sallow hair
Streams on the wind like light,
Cold as a cameo
Her face. They sow a great

Swathe of the plain with dust;
On, on he presses. Now,
Mantles like bellying sails,
They scud at the wood, and so
Storm forward till he reins in—
Midnight upon his brow,

Caparisoned in jet,
Harness, panache of black
Spume-flecked, his stallion's eye
Encrimsoned; — they rein back
To their haunches the quivering steeds
At the brink: — Scrub, tamarack,

Meadows defoliate,
Autumnal. They who have
Outrun the spring, now halt
To seek as in a cheval-
Glass one eternal face.
Each stares at his own self-love.

L'Ile du Levant: The Nudist Colony

All the wide air was trawled for cloud
And then that mass confined in a gray net
And moored to the horizon. Bowed

Down, the golden island under
A dull sky was not at its best; its heyday
Is when the heat crackles, the sun

Pours like a boiling waterfall
On matted underbrush and thicket, on
Boulder, dust; and, over all,

Cicadas at their pastime, drilling
Eyelets of sound, so many midget Singer

78

Sewing machines: busy, then still.
Landing beyond a thorny curve,
We climbed down to the colony, extended
On its plot of beach. In the sudden swerve

Of every eye, they saw as one,
These Nudists on vacation, half their days
Prone, determined as chameleons

To match the ground beneath. At ease
Within a sandy cage, they turned to stare
Up at us clad identities

Who came to stare as openly
As if we too had railings fore and back
And the whole mind of a menagerie.

Such freedom of the flesh, if brave,
Lacks subtlety: a coat of sunburn can
Be badly cut. Well-tailored love

Not only demonstrates but hides,
Not only lodges with variety
But will keep private its dark bed.

We rose: below us golden-brown
Bodies of young and old, heavy and lean,
Lay beached upon the afternoon.

While water, casual as skin,
Bore our departing boat, we saw a form
In relief against the rocky line

And stood to wave farewell from our
World to his, even as charcoal dusk
Effaced his lazy semaphore.

BARBARA HOWES, *a native Bostonian, for four years edited the literary quarterly* Chimera. *Author of two books of poems,* The Undersea Farmer *and* In the Cold Country, *Miss Howes received* Poetry's *Bess Hokin prize in 1949, and was awarded a Guggenheim Fellowship in 1955. Since that time she has been living in Italy with her poet husband, William Jay Smith, and their two small sons.*

Two Somewhat Different Epigrams

I

Oh, God of dust and rainbows, help us see
That without dust the rainbow would not be.

II

I look with awe upon the human race
And God, Who sometimes spits right in its face.

Acceptance

God, in His infinite wisdom,
Did not make me very wise—
So when my actions are stupid
They hardly take God by surprise.

Testament

What shall I leave my son
When I am dead and gone?
    Room in hell to join me
    When he passes on.

What shall I leave my daughter,
The apple of my eye?
    A thousand pounds of salt
    For tears if she should cry.

What shall I leave my wife
Who nagged me to my death?
    I'll leave her more to nag about
    Than she's got breath.

Late Corner

The street light
On its lonely arm
Becomes
An extension
Of the Cross—
The Cross itself
A lonely arm
Whose light is lost.

Oh, lonely world!
Oh, lonely light!
Oh, lonely Cross!

Where? When? Which?

When the cold comes
With a bitter fragrance
Like rusty iron and mint,
And the wind blows
Fresh and sharp as integration
With an edge like gentle apartheid,
And it is winter,
And the cousins of the too thin suits
Ride on bitless horses
Tethered by something worse than pride,
Which areaway, or bar,
Or station waiting room will not say,
Horse and horseman, outside!
With old and not too gentle
Colorless apartheid?

Gone Boy

Playboy of the dawn,
Solid gone!
Out all night
Until 12—1—2 A.M.

Next day
When he should be gone
To work—
Dog-gone!
He ain't gone.

Last Call

I look out into the Yonder
And I don't know where I go—
So I cry, *Lord! Lord!*

Yours is the only name I know.

Some folks might say Your ear is deaf
To one who never called before.
Some folks might say You'll scorn me
Since I never sought Your door.

Yet I cry, *Lord! Lord!*

Lord, that is Your name?

I never knew You,
Never called You.
Still I call You now.

I'm game.

LANGSTON HUGHES *was born in Joplin, Mo., in 1902. He holds both a bachelor's degree and an honorary doctorate from Lincoln University, has held a Guggenheim Fellowship and an American Academy of Arts and Letters grant, and has left almost no form of writing untouched, his published work including poems, short stories, history, juveniles, biography, drama, opera libretti, popular songs, translations, and autobiographies. He lives in New York City.*

JOSEPHINE JACOBSEN

Mollesse

Softly the car goes with the music in it,
Swims softly in the night of boats and stars,
(Begin, begin, but no one will begin it)
The lights ride softly on the rise of spars,
The enormous moon says soft, says soft, says hush.

Drench of fragrance sudden as a touch
Falls from the hidden bush; but softly spoken
The music's syllable says such, and such,
The boats on water where the moon is broken
Sink, softly rise, the fronds brush, softly brush.

The notion of noon, says the palm, was a savage blunder;
There are no prisoners, say the stirring boats in the dark;
(The claves say begin, begin the wonder)
The moon-shot water says, there was never a *shark*:
Of *course* you can keep spring, says the invisible bush.

Short Short Story

Agnes lived with geraniums on the window-sills,
A ginger cat to arch for caresses,
Crisp little bibs on black little dresses
And excellent salads of herbs and cresses;
She was careful with the birthdays of nephews and nieces
    and with Wedgwood and bills.

Agnes' voluble knowledge hobnobbed with psyche and sex:
She knew the causes of early senility
The remotest tribal rites-of-fertility
How the Aztec warriors proved their virility,
And her yellow kitchen was spick, and span was her Celotex.

Agnes knew the thicket where the psychosomatic malingers,
The root that the rat of fear is nibbling
The secret hate of sibling for sibling,
She took her incest without any quibbling
And she blushed to the roots of her hair when the postman
    touched her fingers.

The Eyes of Children at the Brink of the Sea's Grasp

The eyes of children at the brink of the sea's
Grasp, dilate, fix; their water-sculpted hair
Models their heads; crouching a little they stare
In motionless ecstasy of panic

As the upreared load, tilting, tilting titanic
Pitches and shocks them in a rainbow crash
And is upon them with a cat's flash
Before the nearest shrieks and flees.

Most true terror carries them high to us
Up sand as white and dry as safety—thereafter
Gooseflesh and shudders rack them to drunken laughter.
They reel, self-conscious, pantomiming . . .

But presently sober, cautious down the shining
Dark slope of invitation, outward, to the prize
Of shaping danger they go—and widen their eyes
Innocent and voluptuous.

JOSEPHINE (Mrs. Eric) JACOBSEN *was born in Coburg, Canada,
in 1908. She has published three books of poetry,* Let Each
Man Remember, For the Unlost, *and* The Human Climate. *Her
work has appeared in many magazines, not only in this country,
but in England, France, and Ecuador. Mrs. Jacobsen is poetry
critic for the* Baltimore Evening Sun. *During the winter she
lives in Baltimore, and in the summer in Whitefield, N. H.*

WALTER H. KERR

Villanelle

The woods we're lost in aren't real.
We fear success and so we hide.
We lose because we fear to win.

We either stand or else we kneel.
On either hand we bow to pride.
The woods we're lost in aren't real.

The hunter sends a bulletin:
The prey is bent on suicide.
We lose because we fear to win.

Our secret self we can't conceal.
Doc Jekyll says his name is Hyde.
The woods we're lost in aren't real.

The paper tigers shed their skin.
Our fear is never justified.
We lose because we fear to win.

Our compass is a prayer wheel
Whose turning takes us for a ride.
The woods we're lost in aren't real.
We lose because we fear to win.

Curtains for a Spinster

The curtains are of lace, softening darkness
for the one-eyed Clotho at the end of her thread,
at the tag end of a long and winding day.
The wind puffs the fabric into a face,
tracing softly the handiwork of love,
and subsides, leaving a ghost in petit point
like a trace of a vanished breath.

The Proud Trees

A thin rank at regular intervals lines
Curb; being neither at ease nor attention
But somewhere serenely between, being a green
Contemplation but not of our gasoline trance,
Not of the mad dance of our infantile crusades.

They observe a slower procession through our blur
Of limbs as through the blade of a fan; look
Inward contemplating rings like navels,
And feel their timeless bark as soft as fur,
And bare their leaves at suntigers passing by.

Theirs is a different world and a different time.
They are out of phase even with the birds
And, except for a current of windstorm and the common
Transformer of earth, are completely alien to our
Thought, completely escape our words.

I have seen them in the cemeteries,
With their inscrutable look and their sinister roots,
Gazing calmly over the marble silences
And suddenly I have come to believe in kobolds
And hamadryads, in God, and the proud enigmatic angels.

The Dignity of Man—Lesson #1

The tiger, when a man goes by,
Trembles in his stripéd skin
And never meets him eye to eye.

The eagle goes into a spin
To see the Wrights at Kitty Hawk
Blueprint wings from aspirin.

Some creatures like the greater auk
And dinosaur have died of shame,
And some like parrots hide in talk.

The polar bear is cold and tame
To man disguised as Esquimaux
And shoulders all the harpoon blame.

The fox learns from the tally ho
The classic posture of the plays
In the game of human touch and go.

The rats turn slowly in their maze.
A man is more than corridors
Of skin and bone and ricochets.

A man is made of Salvadors,
Of star and sword, of Will and Can,
A man is made of conquerors.

The tiger trembles when a man
Crosses his meridian.

WALTER H. KERR *was born in Indianapolis, Ind., in 1914. His poems have appeared in many magazines in this country and Canada, not to mention Japan, and some have been translated into Japanese. He lists his occupation as printer in the employ of the U.S. Government; is incumbent President of the Federal Poets, a group of poets in the Washington, D.C., area; and makes his home in Hyattsville, Md.*

GALWAY KINNELL

Full Moon

The day is ours together.
The moon of our simple knowledge
That was a half moon
Tonight doubles at the full.

Girl of gentle weather,
May the moon on our new village
Send a fair light down
And bid the dawn stand still

Until each thing is another
And there is nothing for a wedge
Between halves of a moon
That rides all night at the full.

Near Barbizon

At first I thought some animal, wounded,
Thrashed in the brush, for the hunting horns
Had sounded last night and this morning.
No, it was only the little woodgatherer
Out after lunch for twigs for the fire.
He had his own way of breaking a branch.
Others might have laid it across two rocks
And jumped in the middle. He lifted it like a flail
And beat the rocks until the weapon broke.
We talked. Since it was election time I asked
Whom he was voting for. He screwed his eyes.
"If there came into your house by night
Thieves, to which would you offer your wife?"
Whacks he laid on the rock until the branch gave.
"I am too honest, *merde*, or too poor to vote.
There's fuel on the forest floor still."
"What's your trade?" I asked. "Gardener."
"You make things bloom?" "Yes, and the pay's
Nothing." I thought, and the rewards of spirit?
He was flailing the rock in savage, measured

88

Strokes. "The pay's nothing," he repeated,
Looking up without ceasing his labor, keys of both
Eyes flashing: this intellectual, this rich American, this
    fascist boss!

Told By Seafarers

It is told by seafarers
To children who would go to sea,
When the moon on the sea
Lies full, it is then the life-bearers

Abound in the deep, and a pillar
From the rocking sea
Rises, as the god sea
To the moon becomes the straight sailor.

Fair girl — here on the grasses
Of afternoons, as on a sea-
floor grasses wave in the sea,
Lying together in this grass oasis,

We teach you how the sea rises
And the grass teems in the sea
When a moon lies full on the sea
As tell the seafarers, in the sea's disguises.

Leaping Falls

The morning of the winter's
Coldest day, I tried
In desperate concentration
To read Saint Paul,
But though I clung to the words
They whirled and hurled me out.

And so it was I sheered,
Eccentric, into
Outer space,
And tracked with my paces
The forgotten journey of a child
Across the creaking snow,

Up the deer-trail,
Beyond the idled sawmill,
Over the snowdrifted hill

Into the country where
A boy once climbed, and found
The gorge of Leaping Falls.

I thought back on boyhood
And summer, on the rock-shelved
Falls as once they were,
Routing from ledge to ledge,
A tumult at sunrise, the school
And the pageant of my days.

Now they were draped
Without motion or sound,
Icicles fastened in stories
On stillness and rock. Underneath
A heap of icicles broken
Lay dead blue on the snow.

Cold was through and through,
Noiseless. Nothing, nothing
Save clouds at my nostrils
Motioned. Then I uttered a word,
Softly a bleak word
Slid from the lips; at which

A topmost icicle came loose
And fell, and struck another
With a bell-like sound, and
Another, and the falls
Leapt at their ledges, ringing
Down the rocks and on each other

Like an outbreak of bells
That rings and ceases.
The silence turned around
And was silence again.
Beneath the falls on the snow
A twigfire of icicles burned pale blue.

GALWAY KINNELL *was born in 1927 in Pawtucket, R. I. Poems
by him have appeared in* New World Writing, The New Yorker,
Poetry, *and other magazines. He has just returned from a two-
year residence in France, where he has been teaching at the
University of Grenoble.*

CAROLYN KIZER

What the Bones Know

Remembering the past
And gloating at it now,
I know the frozen brow
And shaking sides of lust
Will dog me at my death
To catch my ghostly breath.

I think that Yeats was right,
That lust and love are one.
The body of this night
May beggar me to death,
But we are not undone
Who love with all our breath.

I know that Proust was wrong,
His wheeze: love, to survive
Needs jealousy, and death
And lust, to make it strong
Or goose it back alive.
Proust took away my breath.

The later Yeats was right
To think of sex and death
And nothing else. Why wait
Till we are turning old?
My thoughts are hot and cold.
I do not waste my breath.

Afterthoughts of Donna Elvira

You, after all, were good.
Now it is late, you are kind.
Never too late, to my mind.
The mind catches up with the blood.

You, it is good to know,
Now we are not in thrall,

To me were as kind as you would,
Being the same to all.

Those that are true to one
Love not themselves, love none.
Loving the one and many,
You cannot be true to any.

True to your human kind,
You seemed to me too cruel.
Now I am not a fool,
Now that I fear no scorn,

Now that I see, I see
What you have known within:
Whenever we love, we win,
Or else we have never been born.

To My Friend, Behind Walls

Who will protect you from the thrust of wings,
The bats, the birds, their rustlings, their clamor?
Frenzied, you scrape at droppings, gauze and webs,
And scar your naked face with your own claws:

The face of your first self that chokes on plaster
As the old mansion crumbles, crumbles. *Mother!*
My madness hates you! So the tired self-stalker
Creeps through a passage, yearning for the blast.

A thousand fuses gleam like candelabra,
And one poor shaking hand is too confused
To touch them off. Unlit, they rise and hiss,
Writhe and turn black, and spring above Her brow.

Medusa! There are faces in Her hair!
But you are bandaged: mummified and trussed,
Set in the rocker, told to think it over.
You stare at the scarred and cracking nursery walls,

Cannot spit out the gag when father comes,
Smiling and vague, to change his coat for supper.
At the door, his hand flickers a salutation.
He moves, and he is swallowed by The Voice

Murmuring behind walls the obscene endearments,
The sad, domestic lies: *she was bad again.*
And the bats beat on the window; owls and night-hawks
Pounce in the dark on soft young animals.

The wind is an enemy, a branch tapping Her code.
The window thunders, and the harsh bird voices,
The menace of wings . . . *Nurse, will you hold me?*
So you embrace: *Ah, Love! At last!* Betrayed!

Arms pinioned to your back . . . the canvas hurts!
Defeat, like a hypodermic, floods your veins.
And the jail is calm and soundproof. Heads in wings,
Or upside-down, they doze behind the walls.

CAROLYN KIZER *was born in Spokane, Wash., in 1924 and now lives in Seattle. She published a poem in* The New Yorker *at the age of seventeen and has since appeared in* Poetry, Harper's Magazine, *and* Botteghe Oscure, *among others.*

G. STANLEY KOEHLER

New construction:
Bath Iron Works

It is a crude thing as it shapes up here.
Out of the iron plates' right-angledness
what form, or what movement can be envisioned?

Wrangled somehow together, can you picture
these squares maneuvering with a fleet's grace,
turn after turn, in foaming execution?

Perhaps the secret is not in the form,
but in the gauge. Three quarters inch at most,
vulnerable to gain *élan* and trust

the ocean top for swiftness and delight.

But there are other things to explain.
Laid down on ways inclining toward the river,
its keel was never level, and with each

access its yearning grew, a kind of launching
had begun already. For the shrewd metal
knows where it is, and on the high old timbers

whose foot is in the stream, it feels a current
drawing it down on ways that break the back
quicker than oceans or the cold Kennebec;

in whose waters, could we but catch the season,

we'd shock the pieced-out thing into one weld,
given to the river in a curl of steam.
Proud queen of paradox, who could bind all

angles to the beauty of that profile,
and from the delicate armor's great risk
pluck out such buoyant poise, it is our flaw

in you that fails; for else why should it be
that launched you are a troubling thing to see?
On the calm river the iron floats musing,

and yet we do not take her in that stance.

But when she is heavy laden and sinks
like our hearts with what she carries, then we
shall call her worthy; and for destroyers perfect.

Siciliana:
The landings at Gela

At its own distance
Sicily was sleeping.
Except for fishermen
trolling there was nothing doing.
Fish swam from the nets, and, of course,
all surface disturbances.

On the beaches a bit of horseplay,
vehicles in a pretended war; but this
at a distance. Further on,
along thin roads, under the hills a few
curious gathered in the sun.
Not very many.

How did it come that
with one more sun
the nets would troll iron and tear
through minefields, swaying
in rhythm, the fish
swim out of sight?

On the practice beach
the show improves.
Between sky and water
a fleet unfolds its wake
at one speed. Men take the sun;
nothing could be more southerly.

Ground swell

After the experience of waves
comes this rhythm. The sea is never
so beautiful as on these occasions
when freed of trouble that is not
its own, it runs in slow swells
from the scene of its affliction.

Flexible as the sky to be stirred, and
stirring, the tragic sea in passion
substantial as the earth's moves outward
from anger into this order; largo
for all in nature that can
by so deep strings be shaken.

Tremors that shook it; irrelevant airs
imposing their alien will have passed.
Still that deep reluctance to trouble
is troubled, and moves
as if it would always move, to inner
music, and of its own passion.

G. STANLEY KOEHLER, *born in West Orange, N. J., in 1915, served in World War II as communications officer on destroyers. Holding degrees from Princeton and Harvard, he is now Associate Professor of English at the University of Massachusetts. Previous publication by Mr. Koehler includes poems in* Sewanee Review, Yale Review, *and* Poetry.

KIM KURT

The Sun-Bather

Sleek and lax as a slug in the grass
My sun-browned, oiled down body lies
Where I dropped it flat
And falls from thought.

Under my eyelids the light is ochre
Spinning to black; the outside fever
Of objects is broken,
As knowledge forgotten,

And all sense sinks. I lose my name
Where the blade and bug-leg tickles numb
My slumbered legs
Beyond response.

It seems a way of going back.
As freely as vapor escaping rock
Climbs to pure
Incorporate air,

So my hot body, flat to the green,
Feels sun-dispersed as a thing unborn;
Though gravity-held,
I lie unselved.

Runaway

In snorts of wind, the tawny meadow
Flexes sun like the muscle ripple
Of some full-blooded horse, all supple
To run the whole sky-course to shadow
And leap the dark. Up on an arch
Of hill, my fists are deep in a mane
Of grass, as if to feel the strain
Of an untame earth beneath my touch.
I know I only stay this mount
As it charges stars and splits the days

97

To dust, by the hard grip of my knees
And hands; and whether this is a hunt
Or race, I'm on for a headlong ride.
May all my bareback luck run high
To hold this rampant earth, and fly
My love on the strength of its out-bound stride.

Vernal Paradox

We waited out the lion weeks
Of too much savage March
As some men wait millenniums;
Keeping a hopeful watch
On greyed oak twigs and backyard mud,
Gladly divining green
Before it came. We took the storms
That spit down sleet with rain
As simply part of the same high plan
That drove our smutted sun
Toward equinox, though still no crocus
Broke. The vernal line
Seemed almost sky-inscribed, some gate
That on the twenty-first
We'd pass through with the mounting sun
To feel the lamb days burst.
But when we woke that crossing dawn,
Cold cloud had shut us out
From any prophecy but snow,
And willows cringed in wait
As for a blow. Whatever course
The fled sun kept, it kept
Alone, we guessed; it couldn't climb
For us, if sap was stopped
Near zero. We could retract our hopes
As well as the clamping buds,
And turn again to telling time
By earth's uncertain seeds.

Woodlore

No path at all goes somewhere.
Ask deep woods direction,
And watch how the place most clear
Of clumps leads on; the inflection
Of a shadow goes before
You like a half-thought question,
And half toward answer, you move.
Each turn seems to be verging
Greener than that you leave,
And though your brambled barging
May startle the sun's own dove
From her nest, shape your ranging
Beyond the flush of chance.
Where bog and cat-briar hide
The path from vision, guess
Them through; one plunge may find
The thinnest deer-track prints,
Or a midwood trail ahead.

KIM KURT *was born in 1936 in New Haven, Conn., and since the age of one has lived on Long Island. She has recently completed her junior year at Wellesley. She held the Eleanor Frost Poetry Scholarship at the Bread Loaf School of English in 1956 and has appeared in New World Writing.*

RICHMOND LATTIMORE

The Father

With full acknowledgment to Janet Flanner's "Profile,"
Part 1, *The New Yorker*, March 9, 1957

*They say the phoenix arrives at the time when his father
dies*. Herodotus.

Once a gay wit, subsequently a wretched instructor
with his lilacs and pigeons painted for the Malaga
    bourgeoisie;
even these painted no longer when the unbelievable son

was thirteen, and the brushes handed to him; the little
    teacher
relapsed to being Señor Ruiz, father to one who will not
perpetuate the name of Ruiz, but goes as Picasso

after the warm mother he liked. In the new universe
of meagre blue harlequins, angled cubes becoming
musicians, bitterly sharpened bulls, and naked

desirable shapes of what age makes for consolation,
where will you find the pigeons or the lilacs, where
    handle
the brown feathers of such a bird as fathered this
    phoenix?

Ship Bottom

How gay those bulks that tattered,
years gone, the lace of the blue giant. How gay,
in the Gulf Stream's film of pale calm, scattered
sea monsters at play
off the v of the prow's cool move. Now, shattered,

the giant's toys rot, sanded
and strewn. Oak ribs brown
in air, re-enact on dry water the landed

whale's grin and gasp, as if speared bulks drown
for sky in the lungs and die stranded.

Ship bones commemorate dead toys hurled
ashore by angry blue, time
sands their smash. Far out, still, leviathans, swirled
in the swim of trans-Atlantic tides, climb
the arc of the world.

Max Schmitt in a Single Scull

How shall the river learn
its winter look, steel and brown, how shall we
upon our moving mirror here discern
the way light falls on bridge and bare tree
except as in the painting? Cold fires burn

autumn into winter. Here still
the pencilled sculls dip, precise arms beat
the water-circles of their progress. Skill
arrowheads elegance. City Line to 30th Street
is forever, Eakins, your Schuylkill

and ours. What you had done
made us see what we saw. Thus our eyes
after your image catch the steel and brown
of rowers on the water, improvise
by you our colors in the winter sun.

RICHMOND LATTIMORE *was born in 1906. He is Professor of
Greek at Bryn Mawr College, has published translations of
Greek poetry, including the* Iliad *and various plays, and has
contributed poetry to various magazines. His collected poems
are being published by the University of Michigan Press.*

A Poor Relation

In her coffin, satin-shirred,
Aunt Ellie smiles, four-score and five,
Her grey hair curled, nails manicured,
As never when she was alive.

Mourners gather round to see
Aunt Ellie decked in lace and mauve,
Banked by their flowery charity
As she had never been, alive.

Because their guilt or vanity
Makes such a splurge of pomp and love,
Perhaps Aunt Ellie smiles to see
What she had never, when alive.

The Cemetery Is

A ground of contradictions, where motif
Of human memory enduring grief
Defines by opposites: beside the chaste
Stone the brightest flowers may be placed;
Here granite angels' shadows may transgress
On levelled graves that would be shadowless;
Beside the living green the paper wreath;
A graven hope above, the worm beneath.

But finest marble equals poorest clay
When brief and infinite are held at bay.
The cemetery is . . . to circumvent
The darkness of the grave with bright intent.

Invalid

While this night I read, I'm battleground
For coughs and capsules, aches and shawls,
Pain and poetry, and a will to convalesce
Opposing warm surrender.
Out in the street, wheels depress
The skulls of moonlit snow; the wind
Wastes arrows upon my shield of walls.

So besieged and tenable I assume
Those poets' ills and burdens bound
In more than many a recent poem,
Sink to their common gender
Only to rise, a faint Phoenix, to air
More loving, less suited to despair—
Or is it that I spurn their faulty ground?

The broken swords unearthed, old ploughshares,
And our fathers' sins, monuments of weight
That poets now divide with all:
Let any man be branded ill who dares
Refuse his share of rubble; let his gall
Earn him a deal of hate . . .
Our fathers' guilt becomes our guilty splendor.

Oh, to put down these ruins that mold
The shape of love to such deformity, that breed
Our shames—words, get off my back! I need
More than my sickly flame
To see their end; and welcome the untender
Winter moon whose light through glass falls cold
And healing upon this festering of blame.

AUDREY *(Mrs. Curtiss)* MCGAFFIN *was born in 1914 in Baltimore, Md., her current residence. She has published poems in* Imagi, Voices, Talisman, Whetstone, Shenandoah, The Pound Newsletter, *and other magazines. Her poetry has won several national awards. A first book of poems,* The Imagined Country, *was published this year.*

PHYLLIS McGINLEY

Saint Francis Borgia
or
A Refutation for Heredity

In the Courts of Evil
Borgias dine,
Toasting the Devil
In his own wine,
And while advances
The fiery Shade,
They speak of Francis
The renegade—
Spanish Francis,
Sport of the clan,
Born both Borgia and God-struck Man.

Doom falls shortly,
But where is he—
Francis the portly
Great Grandee?
Schooled to administer
Fief and field,
With two bars sinister
On his shield,
Life-long shaken
By the Borgia pride,
He might be quaffing at Caesar's side.

Yonder, instead,
At peace he sits,
Breaking his bread
With the Jesuits,
Staking his chances
On Christian grace—
White-sheep Francis
With the Borgia face;
Of the family temper
And the family taint,
Shaping a genial Borgia saint.

When, lost and evil,
At dark of the moon,
Supping with the Devil
From a very short spoon,
Gather the Borgias, shorn of hope,
(Soldier and sovereign and fat, false Pope)
They speak of Francis, and wrathful still,
They mock God's mercy
And they curse Free Will
Till wits go reeling
And thunder rolls.

But Francis, kneeling
Prays for their souls.

Literary Landscape with Dove and Poet

The pedant dove, the poet who admires him,
Are adepts, both, of a most natural style.
Each is aware that music needs no meaning.

"Coo, coo," observes the dove all morning long;
All morning long, all evening longer still.
Mourning and evening are his occupations.

While underneath his eaves of occupation,
Dove-plump with melody, the poet murmurs
"Coo, Coo," incessant as a chime of bills.

Each is aware that music needs no meaning
Since the instructed and submissive ear
Believes the Word. "Coo, Coo" is Metaphysics.

A Certain Age

All of a sudden bicycles are toys,
Not locomotion. Bicycles are for boys
And seventh-graders, screaming when they talk.
A girl would rather
Take vows, go hungry, put on last year's frock
Or dance with her own father
Than pedal down the block.

This side of childhood lies a narrow land,
Its laws unwritten, altering out of hand,
But, more than Sparta's, savagely severe.
Common or gentry,
The same tabus prevail. One learns by ear
The customs of the country
Or pays her forfeit here.

No bicycles. No outcast dungarees
Over this season's round and scarless knees,
No soft departures from the veering norm.
But the same bangle
Marked with a nickname, now, from every arm
Identically must dangle,
The speech be uniform—

Uniform as the baubles round the throat,
The ill-made wish, the stiffened petticoat,
And beauty, blurred, but burning in the face.
Now scrubbed and scented
They move together toward some meeting place,
Wearing a regimented
Unutterable grace.

They travel rapt, each compass pointing south—
Heels to the shoes and lipstick on the mouth.

Fourteenth Birthday

The Enemy who wears
Her mother's usual face
And confidential tone
Has access; doubtless stares
Into her writing case
And listens on the phone.

There is no safety. Spies
Who call themselves her betters
Inform by night and day—
Herself the single prize.
Likely they read her letters
And bear the tale away,

Or eavesdrop on her sleep
(Uncountered and unchidden)
To learn her dreams by heart.
There is no lock can keep
A secret rightly hidden
From their destructive art.

But till the end is sure,
Till on some open plain
They bring her to her knees,
She'll face them down—endure
In silence and disdain
Love's utmost treacheries.

PHYLLIS MCGINLEY *was born in Oregon in 1905, is married, has two children, and lives in Larchmont, N. Y. She has published seven books of poetry, including* The Love Letters of Phyllis McGinley, *which won the Edna St. Vincent Millay Award and the Catholic Writers' Guild Award in 1954. She is a member of the National Institute of Arts and Letters.*

VINCENT McHUGH

The Natural History of Pliny

> *Plinny sheweth all*
> *In his story naturall . . .*

What is the sound of the earth spinning?
said Pliny. A vast harmonious roar
too ponderous for the ear to sing?
Do the stars give off a tinkling?
Is there someone at the door?

What is the source of the wind's blowing?
said Pliny. The famous breath of space
whirling the universe in a ring?
Is there no end to wondering?
Why do I watch your face?

The Mice at the Door

Impossible the years have fled away so fast!
    a snake into his hole
    bird into his box
    the voice of his doll
    back into the ventriloquist

Before one could say *eheu*
it was already *fugaces:*
    the bills unpaid
    the notes due
    the works uncollected

and the mice at the door
    in pleated shirts from Brooks Brothers
    and the most effortless dinner jackets,
    saying:
      'If you're going our way, McHugh,
      'we can drop you off
        'ANYWHERE
        'anywhere
         'anywhere
          'anywhere
           'anywhere'

Even yesterday
it was only yesterday:
    all the houses had paint on them
    and a star burned a hole in my vest,
    out of which came a light,
    saying:
        'This man
        'is immortal'

Amphimachos the Dandy

Amphimachos, old Homer's fool,
strolled into battle girt in gold
A dandy of the Karian school,
he made a pool of bold
coruscation amidst the bronze,
as who should say: 'For me the day
'is enough. Let the cold wands
'of the enemy strike. I act the play—

'a dawdling heresiarch,
'the figurative hero, bright
'in one day's battle. The rest dark
'endless grievance, blood and night,
'and the horses plunging'
                    So he went down

the dry river like a sun,
indifferent, to wade and drown
before the day was well begun

A fool? Achilles thought him so
and struck him lifeless with a clang,
and took his shell like a crab's, to glow
in the hero's tent

                The shouts rang,
but not for Amphimachos, who
confused the drama with the true

The Mantis Friend

I had a friend: or thought I had a friend:
a praying mantis. He came at a time
of miscellaneous outrage without end:

like this or any other mortal time
How did I know he was my friend? I did not know:
I thought him so: he made the climb

each day to my apartment on the park: rose
with his equipment like an early aeronaut's:
lettuce-green, reckless of sparrows, all those

seventeen stories to my windowsill: and there
he sat, with not a word out of him. A more profound
chat I can't remember: he was heir

to all the multiguity of silence: not shy,
he made the windowsill his Porch and Garden:
gave me his profile, one attentive eye:

hardly moved, except to demonstrate some points
requiring mathematics: then he made the figures
in the air. He had rather baroque joints,

but no more so than mine: a sharp fork
to the elbow: indeed we resembled each other
in more than a taste for silence in New York

I don't know how I knew he was *he* and not *she:*
I suppose because I could not imagine a *she*
flying up seventeen stories to see me:

but other reasons too: a certain profound
reflective willingness to take a chance
on things likely to get a man off the ground

and into trouble. I offered him food:
even a little wine, to drink or bathe in:
but he was never in the mood; he preferred to brood
110

O we had excellent times together,
speculating on each other's qualities and fate
He dropped round in any kind of weather,

but the sun suited him best: it nourished
his thought like a plant: he *was* a kind of plant,
like you or me, and in the sun he flourished

But vegetative, no: he had the habit and curse
of thought: a great talent for it:
I have known many a man did worse

My questions, I remember, were all ontological:
Why was he he and I I?
Was each of us to himself the end of all?

To all of which he did not answer a word:
nor did I speak one, for that matter
But I knew by the way his eye stirred

he had considered them all and found them fruitless:
a new kind of philosopher, who made
being his ontology, and found no redress

for it, or any compensation when it's gone
Being was a kind of song to him,
though he could not sing, except in being born

One day he flew away: I made inquiry
of the high sky, the policeman, the newsdealer on the corner:
none of them had seen him anywhere nearby

So I lost a friend. I thought of him in the snow
and wondered where a praying mantis would go:
I suppose where all the rest of us must go

VINCENT MCHUGH *was born in Providence, R. I., in 1904. His
novels include* I Am Thinking of My Darling *and* The Victory.
He has recently written a verse play, The Women of Lemnos,
*and is working on a novelette and a long cycle in polyschematist
verse. He lives in San Francisco, Calif.*

111

MARIANNE MOORE

Values in Use

I attended school and I liked the place—
grass and little locust-leaf shadows like lace.

Writing was discussed. They said, "We create
values in the process of living, daren't wait

their historic progress." Be abstract
and you'll wish you'd been specific; it's a fact.

What was I studying? Values in use
"judged on their own ground." Am I still abstruse?

Walking along, a student said offhand,
" 'Relevant' and 'plausible' were words I understand."

A pleasing statement, anonymous friend.
Certainly the means must not defeat the end.

NOTE: Stories are judged at *Partisan Review* by these tests:
maturity, plausibility, relevance of the point of view. The
approach between literature and politics cannot be solved
in abstract fashion. We produce values in the process of
living. The work of art must be appraised on its own ground.
—Philip Rahv, July 27, 1956, in Alston Burr Hall, Cambridge.

MARIANNE MOORE *was born in St. Louis, Mo., in 1887. Her
books include* Observations, What Are Years, Nevertheless,
Collected Poems, Predilections *(essays) and a translation of
the fables of La Fontaine. Miss Moore won the Dial Award in
1924, and has subsequently added to her laurels the Harriet
Monroe Award, the Bollingen Prize, the National Book Award
and the Pulitzer Prize, not to mention Honorary Doctorates in
Literature from Wilson College, Mount Holyoke College, Dick-
inson College, and the University of Rochester. She lives in
Brooklyn.*

112

HERBERT MORRIS

The Road

I like the story of the circus waif
bought by the man-of-weights to be his mistress,
Profit the demon dragging her to market
and Lust the soul who paid in lire for her.

I like the peculiarities of her faith,
the startling quality of that innocence,
kissing the hand that dealt her cruelty
believing, poor and dumb, that this was love.

I relish a destitution stripped to sing
pure in a voice all passion and denial:
such are the driven burning by their breath
more than mere air allows and cold permits.

I savor my own involvement and concern
lest all the transformations seem unreal,
lest love be painted water-sweet and classic
rather than salt and anguish to the end.

I like her squatting in the village road
combing the dust for something of her own,
coming away belonging and committed,
roots to be cherished, stones she could befriend.

And what I like the subtlest and profoundest
is that the circus traveled grief to grief,
educating the waif into a woman
loving and beautiful and fiercely proud.

I think of the sense of fury in that road,
stooping to scratch the earth out for a life
somewhere awaiting finding in one's name.
I like that, and I like the word Expense.

I think of the years together which they had,
the strong-man working her into the act,
that hint, despite himself, of some devotion.
I like that, and I like the ring of Cost.

Not in a root, or stone, but in a man
she found a thing to hold her tenderness.
I like her dedication after that,
her saying, if she spoke, I live by this.

And what I like pervasive and forever
is that my eyes have wept the tale before,
wanting the telling not so much as story
but for the way the waif befits my life.

Workmen

Five workmen hired here to shovel dirt
have passed among them some milk-bottle of
cool water which I felt flowed more like love,
a drinking whose raw beauty fully hurt.

Each mouth touched where the other four had been:
that of itself spoke such humanity
as to have made it inescapably
devotions of my own I struggled in.

Imagine that pure structure on the day
as lemons on a beach, a house of sand,
a coolness in the desert that one's hand
beautifully caused to blossom from decay.

That was the way, that was the wealth of way
they spent and went in water man to man,
common and strong and world to understand.
That was their way, and this is what we pay

in learning understanding from those five:
envy that summer touches them to thirst
for gifts of back-lot water, and this first
sheer pain that drinking means to be alive.

The North of Wales

I met the yawning of my appetite
this morning when they entered and we spoke,
music and early waking and the sea.
Had you vast beaches in the north of Wales?:
purest wild strips of inlet where the sand
sank to a loam that richly fed green fir,
and waters of a midnight mooned and starred
beyond the mind's small vision of a light.

I groomed the splendor of my hungering
and hungered splendored in the spread of it
this morning where they laid me ample food,
youngness and blonde with strength and that sheer line
of eye, of lip, of liquid-clearest hand,
that flickered roaring from their blaze of health,
high fires of early wakings by the sea.

So that I saved my remnant bitter tea,
my driest toast, that it enable me
to feel them longer and luxuriate,
softly and striving while a rain began,
among the weathers of their loveliness.

The Brahms

Leaflight to lamplight, blind with so much sight,
turn pages for me, modest with delight:
Scarlatti through the morning, Brahms by night.

Light me the pages fired by your hands
brighter than all the lamplight understands
and quite beyond what melody demands.

Higher than candelabra, deep as psalms,
I'll play the long and darkest songs of Brahms:
what more is evening than what night becalms?

Starlight and moonlight quiet at your throat,
we'll weave the strands of music like a coat
brilliant and warm about us, note for note.

These are the gifts I mustered in this room,
not sonatinas nor some rigadoon,
but Brahms tonight, Schumann this afternoon.

These are the sounds I mastered for your ear,
profoundest phrase and chording coming clear
above the lovely Brahms which you could hear.

This is the self I spoke from sheaves you turned,
seated beside me where the lamplight yearned
richer and truer toward the wealth you burned.

Twilight to midnight, turn me pages long:
how late it is, but, bone for bone, prolong
the whiteness of your body in the song.

HERBERT MORRIS *has appeared in* Poetry, Accent, *the* Kenyon,
Sewanee, Paris, *and* Western *reviews, among others. He is in
his twenties and was born in New York.*

LISEL MUELLER

Sans Souci

(Frederick the Great's summer palace near Potsdam)

It does not make sense in terms of historical fact,
The unabashed gesture, the celebration of joy,
Birds that catch and diffract
The afternoon sun and drink from a bubbling nymph
Who beckons a marble boy;

Nor the make-believe heaven inside: golden frames
Looping their spiralling curls about mirrors that blaze
Whirlpools of light on the games
Of Arcadian lovers dappling a celadon wall;
Yet we might have expected it. Praise

Is the louder and passion the fiercer for need,
Fiercest when bred in a mind that has knelt to a whip
And recanted its natural creed
Of splendor and bliss. Rigidity once removed
Is freedom and grace, and the tight-stretched line of a lip

Curves to the flute's convolutions of silver and breath.
But for the hair that we split in order to prove
Otherwise, death
Reverses to motion and sunlight. Turned inside-out,
Negation is equal to love.

The People at the Party

They are like tightrope walkers, unable to fall
From the precise thread of their making,
Having achieved the most delicate of all
Balances of the brain, which is forsaking

Joy on the one hand, and on the other, terror;
Holding themselves exquisitely aloof
From the contingencies of love and error,
They dare nothing, are wholly removed

By the will not to suffer, from us who do.
Ah, but they are precariously perched
On their rope of detachment. Who
Can be sure someone improperly coached

Won't say the wrong word or turn back
The cruel joke with a human response?
That the only girl not in serpent black
Will keep her distance? There is always a chance

Someone careless or young will unsettle the cable,
Bring on the vertigo and set them reeling
Toward the sheer drop, toward the unstable
Inexorable wilderness of feeling.

Apples

Light has transformed them. Their utility gone,
they spill at you from a table on which they don't really lie;
you would not dare eat one. Taking one from the group
would rearrange the paper-stiff tablecloth,
call shadows from corners. Each one is needed to keep

the cut primroses and their polished leaves
in a porcelain jug. The proof of the apple
is not in the eating, not in the runaway juice
or the firm flesh. It is in the way the light

fastens to roundness, its orange and yellow grasp
on the reality of the idea of apples.

118

For a Nativity

Look: Florentines and Umbrians have made whole
our nail-pierced son, our disembodied Christ;
he lies newborn among the blessed beasts,
Italy's vineyards at his back and she
his Tuscan mother, on her knees in blue.

Who mixed their colors to these shades of faith
knew that the world turns by an infant's breath
and Bethlehem is the name for any place
where princes sit with oxen, and the meek
lean against peacocks rich with golden tails.

We bend our minds to hear the ass bray out
his joy above the jubilee of kings
and barefoot angels. Stepping across the quick
hoofs of white horses for a closer look,
we lose our crosses in the dancing crowd.

LISEL MUELLER *was born in Hamburg, Germany, in 1924, came to the United States in 1939, and lives in Evanston, Ill. She began writing poetry in 1954, and has appeared in* The New Yorker, Perspective, Talisman *and* Voices.

PHILIP MURRAY

The Locust Hunt

When Fabre took his children locust hunting
Across the stubby meadows of Provence
Young Paul was content to capture the large Grey Locust
Perched like a small bird on the everlastings,
But little Marie-Pauline preferred honey color
And searched hopefully for the rich Italian
With gauzy pink wings and striking carmine legs
Which liked the mulberry bushes best of all;
And on these bushes it was she who caught
In her excited hands the morning's prize,
A great beauty bearing St. Andrew's cross,
That martyr's X, marked on its slender back
By four white slanted stripes, and further patched
With rare Greek green like verdigris on bronze.

How gleefully when they spied one did they scoop
The delicate captive into a paper funnel,
And with what care, approaching tenderness,
Did father place it in a tiny cage,
Promising if the children were sharp hunters
And caught more specimens than he required
They should have locusts for supper,
Prepared the Arab way and served with honey;
It was perhaps a dubious reward
For Fabre said later, cautiously—they were good,
But none of us desired to have them again.

The Cloud of Unknowing

Clouds and darkness are round about Him.
Psalms XCVI 2
By love He may be gotten and holden, but by thought
never.—Walter Hilton

Now shall the body   obey the soul
As the hand governs   and the glove obeys.

Not through the windows   of my wit
Come these sweet stirrings   to be naught
But this little ghost,   clad in undeadliness,
Fixed on this leash   of longing within,
To hang wholly   in this nowhere,
This dark cloud, beating   a blind beholding.

The more I love,   the more I long to love,
Grounded in grace   where all woe is wanting,
No longer festered   in flesh or fantasy
But kissed and clasped   like father and child;
A naked feeling   of my own being
Knitted and knotted   to God Himself only;

Not in congealed vapours,   nor vacant dark
But in this lightsome   unknown knowing,
Crying this one cry: Sin, sin! Out, out!
Until that instant   of full forsaking
When my few words   teem with fruit and fire
Like this word,   GOD,   or this word,   LOVE;

Then, though I am   poured out like water,
I shall spring up,   a sparkle from the coal.

PHILIP MURRAY *was born in Philadelphia, Pa., in 1924. He received an M.A. in Medieval Literature from Columbia University in 1955 and has been teaching at Brooklyn College since 1956. His poems have appeared in* New Poems, *in the* Antioch Review Anthology *and in many magazines.*

LOUISE TOWNSEND NICHOLL

Time in the Sun

I go with earth, experiencing light,
The pure communication of the sun
Which no grammarian could conjugate,
So bright-absorbed and bended into one
Intensive single form, inflectionless,
Are noon and dawn today, and early, late.
This is the tenseless vesture that I wear,
The time in air that turns to timelessness,
The garment without joining or weight
Which goes with earth and is itself the light.

The Made Lake

Bounded unbrokenly by summer weather,
Wearing its sumptuous, eternal look,
The land so widely welded all together
Was interrupted only by the brook.

On this same ground we see but blurred resemblance
To that long cherished green mirage: where once
Was sward now sway the waters of remembrance
On whose new margins children greet the swans.

Improvising

Playing, she puts her instrument to sleep
And traces out the movement of its dream.
Piano and *piano*, she will keep
The state of soft suspension that will break
Only if this strong creature shall awake
And suddenly recount a stranger theme
From deeper levels of its multi-slumber.
And what it says she never will remember.

Incense

The summer as it passes owes to night
The pattern and the progress of its flight,
The flowers which succeed each other turning
As slow as constellations and as sure,
Like those great swinging censers deeply burning,
Dispensing time in sweet sequential shower:
Time the inflammable, the fragrant burden
Of star and flower, in the sky and garden.
The summer is a night, so swiftly slow
Does the one tempo of the movement flow.

Different Winter

As junco is with winter,
White breast against white snow
Blended soft and true,
So, quiet and at one
With climate of my own,
I reach the world's sweet center;
Drifted in different winter,
The stillness gently sown
Till all be blent to one,
I rest as soft and true
As bird that clings to snow.

LOUISE TOWNSEND NICHOLL *was one of the founders of* The
Measure, *one of the more distinguished little poetry magazines
of the twenties. Formerly an associate editor with E. P. Dutton
& Company, she is now an Editor and Literary Advisor in her
own right. Author of a half dozen volumes of poetry, the latest
being* The Curious Quotient, *Miss Nicholl in 1954 was awarded
the Academy of American Poets Fellowship Award. She is now
working on a new book.*

MARY ELIZABETH OSBORN

Exquisite Lady

Say goodnight to him and shut the door,
Shudder at grossness of the human mind;
Yet if you turn your passion toward a star,
Remember that Aldebaran is blind.

Old Man in the Park

Saint Francis? No indeed, although at that
(quick now, sparrows, finish up your bread-crumbs)
perhaps his motive wasn't pure benevolence
any more than mine is. I know why I do it:

if a man's alone he has to talk to something.
The birds are greedy; feed them and they'll swoop
and flutter close and perch and peck and scold
to get full value out of the transaction.

That's all it is to them; but what I gain
is something better, a kind of intimacy,
an easy habit of saying, *brother . . . sister . . .*
You see now what I mean about the saint.

Come Not Near

Sparrows in gossip outside the bedroom eaves
provide ironic awaking on April dawn
to a woman alone whose yearning is set on doves.
Liars . . . she murmurs, closing the window down.

But still she listens in the diminished room
and re-creates a remembered voice to draw
herself from solitude: sudden wings gleam
over her vision, and muted notes come through.

She sees the doves together among the leaves,
conversing without human prevision of loss;
feathered breasts, mate to mate, immaculate lives
transcendent beyond the barrier of glass.

Water-Images
(V.W. 1882-1941)

Mrs. Ambrose watched the iridescence
(looking into the river near Waterloo Bridge)
while a floating piece of straw, riding the current,
whirled and vanished.

Betty Flanders, seated beside the bay,
saw in the quivering tides a premonition:
to Mrs. Ramsay, at the edge of a northern ocean
a lighthouse beckoned.

With the waves—blue and green, sweeping the beach
through the lengthening day, changing, losing color
in the ambiguous night—moved the children's lives,
rhythmic and rompish.

The Pargiters knew their years of unfulfillment;
clouds covered London, autumn ruffled the Channel,
snow clogged the streams whose paths flowed dull beneath
    arches,
muddy and secret.

Let us praise these fragile fictions as more enduring
than the final vision (unguessed-at, unrecorded)
of one who, decision taken, darkly plunged
deep into water.

MARY ELIZABETH OSBORN *was born at Margaretville in the
Catskill Mountains of New York State. In 1955 she published a
novel,* Listen for the Thrush. *She is Professor of English at Hood
College in Frederick, Md.*

ANTHONY OSTROFF

The Sparrows at the Airport

Their brown, harmless flack
Which bursts in feathery chirrupings
About the apron stings
The eye with what they lack

Of speed and power. Their size,
Suitable to glean the crumbs
Of great flight, humdrums
Brown earth into their lives.

Yet over the field they break
Gustily tumbled up to try
Ambitious missions by
Deliberate mistake,

So one must think them pressed
To know the promise if they fall,
The way their careless small
Flight puts it to test.

Meteoric blue
Spans of silver daze the air
About them. Runways flare
To giant craft that prove

Their slight inconsequence,
And all seems scheduled to decree
Their humility
Amid new monuments.

But there, as if to sing
Election from their minute conclave,
They chatter and perch, brave
What short chance may bring,

And watch the liners landing
Safe against imponderable odds,
With quick indifferent nods
And rare understanding.

The River Glideth in a Secret Tongue

By this bright bank the easy noon
Does keep the fisher and his song.
The smallest current speaks.

Brown or green the water moves.
The fisher casts his line for love.
The solstice comes, and lasts.

Alone, where trees stretch deep their roots,
Long lovers lain in touch with depths,
He lays him down in shade

Listening where the silver fish
Unseen explain the water's wash
Of brown and silver age.

The river glideth in a secret tongue.

Where lovers lay ten years ago
The sun gives no command to do.
By water all things grow.

The slow day's celebration spins
Its line about all scenes, and man
Reflects the length of time.

Drawn down to watery shade he hears
No sound but eternal vespers and all
The great riches of tears.

Long fisher in the noon, he lies
Where all his frailest lines are loose,
And finds attachments there.

The river glideth in a secret tongue
And doth flow deep the summer long.

So Long Folks, Off to the War

When I was little, oh a very small boy,
With a Ford, fish, and go fly your kite,
I lived in a house in a cookie jar joy,
With a bed, game, and I'm it tonight.

I wore short pants and had dimples in my knees,
With a Whitney-Pratt, call me that again.
I had a girl friend more pretty than you please,
With a top, bee, and so's your old man.

I played in the street, oh I never saw school,
With a Campbell can, and knock *that* off,
I hid and I sought and I broke THE rule,
With a me, who, and why don't you cough?

When I was happy, oh a very small boy,
With a sink, stove, and jump in the lake,
I made mud huts I would never destroy,
With a strap, please, be good for my sake.

I didn't grow much, and then I grew fast,
With a book, bat, and why don't you try?
I never was first but I was never last,
With a good, bad, and who knows why?

I grew like grass, Oh! we said, Like corn!
With an ache, break, and which way to go?
I dreamed some nights that I'd never been born,
With a glad, sad—I still don't know.

ANTHONY OSTROFF *was born in Gary, Ind., 1923, and educated at Northwestern University, the University of Michigan, the University of Grenoble, and the Sorbonne. Winner of Avery Hopwood Awards in Fiction and Criticism, he has also held fellowships at Yaddo, the Huntington Hartford Foundation, and the University of California's Younger Faculty Fellowship. He has also worked as steel worker, punch press operator, farm hand, salesman, and tavern pianist; at present he is Assistant Professor of Speech in the University of California at Berkeley.*

KENNETH PORTER

Old Thad Stevens
(An American Legend)

Thaddeus Stevens was a burning scandal—
and he put no bushel over the candle!

Gambled all night—in the morning gave
his winnings to a widow or a runaway slave!

His housekeeper's name was Lydia Smith,
a bright mulatto and a cause of myth

and rumor—horrifying all
Southrons remembering the Quadroon Ball!

Bent brow, stern face, gaunt frame, club foot,
Thad was a gnarled old hemlock root—

but deep and strong to feed a tree
whose branches whispered "Liberty!"—

expressed through public education
and universal emancipation.

******

"Forty acres and a mule"
was old Thaddeus Stevens' rule:

"Confiscate the slave-lords' land—
forty acres to each field hand!

"*Pay* for it? *Taxes?* Why you dunce,
Sweat paid for it—more than once!

"For Freedom isn't much," he said,
If you have to beg—or buy—your bread.

"But forty acres and a mule to plow it—
No need to beg or buy—you *grow* it!"

(Corn for bread and corn for hogs—
everything fat—but the possum-dogs!

Plow your own land, tread your own floor—
and a government musket behind the door

for old-time slavers that gits too big
and has to reckon with the Union League!)

*   *   *

But even before Old Thad was dead
most of the misnamed Radicals said

to themselves: "If we confiscate plantations,
what of ourselves and our relations

"should the next on the list be our factories?—
and, with land, the niggers will vote as they please—

"perhaps not even Republican!"
So in the South the Ku Klux Klan

masked and rode and murdered and burned
while the solid Northern citizen turned

to building railroads and looting the Treasury
and at last, with a sigh of relief if not pleasure, he

released the Negro to the shirted bands
and even omitted to wash his hands.

But Thaddeus Stevens, fortunately,
ere this last act of the tragedy—

triumph of allied coward and knave—
lay in his unsegregated grave.

*   *   *

Some day when men have half their evens
we'll dare talk proudly of Old Thad Stevens.

Epitaph for a Man from Virginia City

> Cashed in his chips
>   in '71—
> quicker with cards
>   than with a gun.

KENNETH PORTER, *born in 1905, is co-author of one book of verse,* Christ in the Breadline. *He is a Professor of History at the University of Illinois.*

DACHINE RAINER

Upon Being Awakened at Night by my Four Year Old Daughter

When I consider, Thérèse,
The cricket in its shrill address,
Penetrating your warm, familiar room,
Ceaselessly proclaiming he means no harm:
Who begs release and begs release,

This orthopter in all its fury, Thérèse,
Knows more of fear than you possess,
You, bedded deep in your dense room,
While he, mysteriously bereft of stars—O cease!
Heralds—O won't he cease?—his doom.

Come! let us seek, Thérèse,
His self-imprisonment, and bless
Our certainty that this deep room
Conceals no giant who means you harm:
So mutually arrange our green release.

By your sleep again covered, Thérèse,
Innocent of stress your face marvelous
Lies, unsuspecting what I must confess:
Those things which me most terrify
I neither can hear nor touch nor see.

Night Musick for Thérèse

Upon the black horse of midnight I ride,
Darkness before me and black on my side,
The sky dark above me, the earth far below,
On the black horse of midnight I ride, I ride,
On the black horse of midnight I ride.

Upon the black rocker, drifting asleep
Round arms around me, my dark soul does keep,
Deep feathers drifting, the rocker we ride,
Darkness behind me, and black on my side,
On the black horse of midnight I ride.

This dark song unravelling the blackness like wool,
His thick black mane moving the air at will,
The light heart upon mine, the rocker we ride,
The sky dark above me, the earth far below,
On the black horse of midnight I ride.

Epithalamium for Cavorting Ghosts

Covertly under the line tree aspen,
In brown wood, on the meadow's green toppling plain,
Everywhere and forever we two together: this is the fiction
Which won my dazzled life.

Your brown graceful brow, your wide scrutinizing eyes
—Have I their durability too gravely esteemed?:—
On the rambling earth passionate seasons flower the grass,
We falter and fumble, our shadow wavers.

The bait of your long legged height, the stance of your
    fine words,
Your gracious hands, the seasons tumble to earth
As upon this fumbling earth we rock and topple.
Tippling this fiction, I gratefully drown my life.

For this, husband and child are fleeing, mysterious ghosts,
And I, well married to a remarkable fiction
I riddling make or brooding spend, in which is lost
My only unhoarded life.

Perhaps we wildly turn upon the incomparable ground and
    gasp
At the ferocity of thorns, or blush at the tippled scent of
    marjoram,
Frozen by summer's sun, burning in winter's final blast
I have all sensuous hell to love you in.

DACHINE RAINER *was born in New York City in 1921. Her work is represented in W. H. Auden's* Book of Modern American Verse. *Two published novellas, entitled* A Room at the Inn *and* The Party, *are sections of a projected longer work. With Holley Cantine, she collaborated as editor of* Prison Etiquette, *an anthology of writing by American conscientious objectors, and, also with Mr. Cantine, edits the anarchist quarterly* Retort *and the local weekly newspaper,* The Wasp, *both published in Bearsville, N. Y., where she lives.*

THEODORE ROETHKE

"The Shimmer of Evil"
Louise Bogan

The weather wept, and all the trees bent down;
Bent down their birds: the light waves took the waves;
Each single substance gliddered to the stare;
Each vision purely, purely was its own:
—There was no light; there was no light at all:

Far from the mirrors all the bushes rang
With their hard snow; leaned on the lonely eye;
Cold evil twinkled tighter than a string; a fire
Hung down: And I was only I.
—There was no light; there was no light at all:

Each cushion found itself a field of pins,
Prickling pure wishes with confusion's ire;
Hope's holy wrists: the little burning boys
Cried out their lives an instant and were free.
—There was no light; there was no light at all.

The Sensualists

"There is no place to turn," she said,
    "You have me pinned so close;
My hair's all tangled on your head,
    My back is just one bruise;
I feel we're breathing with the dead;
    O angel, let me loose!"

And she was right, for there beside
    The gin and cigarettes,
A woman stood, pure as a bride,
    Affrighted from her wits,
And breathing hard, as that man rode
    Between those lovely tits.

"My shoulder's bitten from your teeth;
    What's that peculiar smell?

No matter which one is beneath,
    Each is an animal,"—
The ghostly figure sucked its breath,
    And shuddered toward the wall;
Wrapped in the tattered robe of death,
    It tiptoed down the hall.

"The bed itself begins to quake,
    I hate this sensual pen;
My neck, if not my heart, will break
    If we do this again,"—
Then each fell back, limp as a sack,
    Into the world of men.

I Knew a Woman

I knew a woman, lovely in her bones,
When small birds sighed, she would sigh back at them;
Ah, when she moved, she moved more ways than one:
The shapes a bright container can contain!
Of her choice virtues only gods should speak,
Or English poets who grew up on Greek
(I'd have them sing in chorus, cheek to cheek).

How well her wishes went! She stroked my chin,
She taught me Turn, and Counter-turn, and Stand;
She taught me Touch, that undulant white skin;
I nibbled meekly from her proffered hand;
She was the sickle; I, poor I, the rake,
Coming behind her for her pretty sake
(But what prodigious mowing we did make).

Love likes a gander, and adores a goose:
Her full lips pursed, the errant note to seize;
She played it quick, she played it light and loose;
My eyes, they dazzled at her flowing knees;
Her several parts could keep a pure repose,
Or one hip quiver with a mobile nose
(She moved in circles, and those circles moved).

Let seed be grass, and grass turn into hay:
I'm martyr to a motion not my own;
What's freedom for? To know eternity.

I swear she cast a shadow white as stone.
But who would count eternity in days?
These old bones live to learn her wanton ways:
(I measure time by how a body sways).

The Centaur

The Centaur does not need a Horse:
He's part of one, as a matter of course:
'Twixt Animal and Man divided,
His Sex-life rarely is one-sided;
He can, like Doves and Sparrows, do:—
What else he does is up to you.

The Mistake

He left his pants upon a chair:
She was a widow, so she said:
But he was apprehended, bare,
By one who rose up from the dead.

THEODORE ROETHKE *was born in Saginaw, Mich., in 1908. His books of poems are* Open House, The Lost Son and Other Poems, Praise to the End! *and* The Waking; Poems *1933-1953. He has won the Eunice Tietjens and Levenson prizes awarded by* Poetry, *an award of the American Academy of Arts and Letters, and a Guggenheim Fellowship. He is Professor of English at the University of Washington. He won the Pulitzer Prize in 1954.*

MAY SARTON

A Celebration

I never saw my father old;
I never saw my father cold.
His stride, staccato, vital,
His talk struck from pure metal
Simple as gold, and all his learning
Only to light a passion's burning.
So, beaming like a lesser god,
He bounced upon the earth he trod
And people marvelled on the street
At this stout man's impetuous feet.

Loved donkeys, children, awkward ducks,
Loved to retell old simple jokes;
Lived in a world of innocence
Where loneliness could be intense;
Wrote letters until very late;
Found comfort in an orange cat—
Rufus and George exchanged no word,
But while George worked his Rufus purred—
And neighbors looked up at his light
Warmed by the scholar working late.

I never saw my father passive;
He was electrically massive.
He never hurried, so he said,
And yet a fire burned in his head;
He worked as poets work, for love,
And gathered in a world alive,
While black and white above his door
Spoke Mystery, the avatar—
An Arabic inscription flowed
Like singing: "In the name of God."

And when he died, he died so swift
His death was like a final gift.
He went out when the tide was full,
Still undiminished, bountiful;
The scholar and the gentle soul,
The passion and the life were whole.
And now death's wake is only praise,

As when a neighbor writes and says:
"I did not know your father, but
His light was there. I miss the light."

Nativity
Piero della Francesca

O cruel cloudless space,
And pale bare ground where the poor infant lies!
Yet we do feel restored
As in a sacramental place
Transcended by peculiar Grace;
And here a vision of such peace is stored,
Healing flows from it through our eyes.

Comfort and joy are near,
Not as we know them in the usual ways,
Personal and expected,
But utterly distilled and spare
Like a cool breath upon the air.
Emotion, it would seem, has been rejected
For a clear geometric praise.

Even the angels' stance
Is architectural in form,
And they tell no story.
We see on each grave countenance
Withheld as in a formal dance,
The austere joy, the serene glory:
It is the inscape keeps us warm.

Poised as a monument
Thought rests, and in these balanced spaces
Images meditate:
Whatever Piero meant,
The strange impersonal does not relent:
Here is love, naked, lying in great state
On the bare ground, as in all human faces.

MAY SARTON, *born in Belgium in 1912, lives in Cambridge, Mass. The latest of her several novels,* The Birth of a Grandfather, *will appear this year; her fourth book of poetry is* The Land of Silence. *She has received the Golden Rose Award of the New England Poetry Society, Bryn Mawr's Lucy Martin Donnelly Fellowship, and a Guggenheim Fellowship in 1955-56.*

LOUIS SIMPSON

To the Western World

A siren sang, and Europe turned away
From the high castle and the shepherd's crook.
Three caravals went sailing to Cathay
On the strange ocean, and the captains shook
Their banners out across the Mexique Bay.

And in our early days we did the same.
Remembering our fathers in their wreck
We crossed the sea from Palos where they came
And saw, enormous to the little deck,
A shore in silence waiting for a name.

The treasures of Cathay are never found.
In this America, this wilderness
Where the axe echoes with a lonely sound,
The generations labor to possess
And grave by grave we civilize the ground.

The Silent Generation

When Hitler was the Devil
He did as he had sworn
With such enthusiasm
That even, *donnerwetter*,
The Germans say, "Far better
Had he been never born!"

It was my generation
That put the Devil down
With great enthusiasm.
But now our occupation
Is gone. Our education
Is wasted on the town.

We lack enthusiasm.
Life seems a mystery;
It's like the play a lady

Told me about: "It's not . . .
It doesn't *have* a plot,"
She said, "It's history."

Tom Pringle

The May moon rises bright and clear
Across the windowpane,
It brings the flowers every year
But not my loves again.
I too have heard the melody
That lovers like to hear;
I slept, I dreamed in Arcady,
I woke, and it was there.

The joys we had, the joys we miss,
Take all our joy away,
And many who were glad to kiss
Are now content to pray.
Their heaven is a hospital,
Their piety a crutch;
They don't appeal to me at all,
I like the world too much.

I will not jar the stars with praise
In silence as they sing;
To tell eternity to days
Might swerve an angel's wing.
But I will watch the comets' flight
And not a cloud between
From perfect day to perfect night
And wonder what they mean.

Louis Simpson, *born in Jamaica, B.W.I., in 1923, is the author of* Good News of Death and Other Poems. *He has published poetry and criticism in* The Hudson Review, The New Yorker, Partisan Review, The American Scholar, *and other publications. In 1957 he was awarded a Hudson Review Writing Fellowship, and the Prix de Rome.*

Eighteen

It was yesterday she roller-skated down
the rink in bright red jeans; her hair, a po-
ny tail; her song, jazz of the "rollin' houn' "
between the pop of bubble gum.

Tiptoe
in cinderella pumps today, eighteen,
she pulses into June; her delphin dress,
peacocked chiffon; blonde head, a wavy sheen;
and heyday tongue dialed to winsomeness.

Tuxedoed legs glide from a spice brown car;
a door clangs like a bell and taillights blink;
up to our gate no coltish gestures mar
the stride of young maturity.

We think:
Not wholly earth, nor all of heaven, this joy
between our daughter and the neighbor boy.

Land of the Free

Analogous to floral pageantry
of Pasadena float in sunny sky,
up to cathedral steps this Easter day
the preening crowd moves by.

Equal in quality the tiffanied
strut fragilely on lucite heel; both maid
and mistress wear exclusive gown and toque
like peacocks on parade.

Girls from the East Side and the West display
free-enterprise of perfumed elegance
on April Avenue; their labarums
confirm hallmark of France.

Only the usher can discriminate
in democratic throng by telltale hand
ungloved, guarding a costly orchid tuft,
plebeian in our land.

After Mardi Gras

The limousine up to my brass facade
brought tailored glove, whalebone, and miniver;
and to the egg-shell voices with a nod
the porter set the elevator purr.

I bent the knee to bankbills, poured the Scotch,
clanked coin for coin, and whirled along the floor
a can-can dame until the music watch
signalled decanter, crumpet evermore.

Past midnight: quartered slice of Roquefort moon
sparkles the frost outside the casement pane.
Within, the gobletted in lounges croon
denuded of gentility.

                                        Urbane
my reach between cutglass for crystal bowl
to rinse the reek of caviar wed to smoke;
to flutter fingertip in damask scroll;
and all the while from beveled frame, a joke
has glassed the bacchanalian brow of host
with clownish streak of ash.

                        Snores dim the night
and from the fumes, susurrus of a ghost:
Ash trays and ashes, ashen Sybarite.

SISTER MARY HONORA, O.S.F., *holds a B.A. degree from Loras
College, and an M.A. from the Catholic University of America.
She is a member of the Sisters of St. Francis of Mount St.
Francis in Dubuque, Iowa, and for the past six years has been a
teacher at St. Paul High School, Worthington, Iowa.*

WILLIAM JAY SMITH

At the Tombs of the House of Savoy

Turin beneath, on the green banks of the Po,
Lies ringed with bright sunlight, with peaks of snow,
While here in the dark this death's-head wears a crown.
The dead look up, and Death on them looks down,
And bares his teeth, his bone-white haddock eyes,
Which take the casual visitor by surprise
And follow him intently on his round
As fishbone-fine his steps through vaults resound.

Death of a Jazz Musician

I dreamed that when I died a jukebox played,
And in the metal slots bright coins were laid;
Coins on both my eyes lay cold and bright
As the boatman ferried my thin shade into the night.

I dreamed a jukebox played. I saw the flame
Leap from a whirling disk which bore my name,
Felt fire like music sweep the icy ground —
And forward still the boatman moved, and made no sound.

Dead Snake

A gray financier in a thin black auto
Drove over a snake on a country road;
Birds flew up in dust that gathered,
Oak leaves trembled throughout the wood.
Decisive indeed the defeat of Evil;
And inconclusive the triumph of Good.

A Pavane for the Nursery

Now touch the air softly,
Step gently. One, two . . .
I'll love you till roses
Are robin's-egg blue;

I'll love you till gravel
Is eaten for bread,
And lemons are orange,
And lavender's red.

Now touch the air softly,
Swing gently the broom.
I'll love you till windows
Are all of a room;
And the table is laid,
And the table is bare,
And the ceiling reposes
On bottomless air.

I'll love you till Heaven
Rips the stars from his coat,
And the Moon rows away in
A glass-bottomed boat;
And Orion steps down
Like a diver below,
And Earth is ablaze,
And Ocean aglow.

So touch the air softly,
And swing the broom high.
We will dust the gray mountains,
And sweep the blue sky;
And I'll love you as long
As the furrow the plow
As However is Ever,
And Ever is Now.

WILLIAM JAY SMITH, *born in Winnfield, La. in 1918, has published two books:* Poems, *and* Celebration at Dark, *as well as* Laughing Time, *a collection of children's poems. A new book in this category,* Boy Blue's Book of Beasts, *will appear this year, as will* Poems 1947-1957. *A Rhodes Scholar in 1947, Mr. Smith has also translated and edited Valery Larbaud's* Poems of a Multimillionaire, *and* Selected Writings of Jules Laforgue. *With his wife, poet Barbara Howes, and their two small sons, he has spent the past two years in Italy.*

MARVIN SOLOMON

The Giraffe

To show that Africa is more than breadth
And width, is height and disappearing views;
To prove exception, is the bright giraffe.
He grazes broccolied acacias
And aerial alfalfas with a stiff
But justified hauteur. His motion is
Of caravels and marvels. And, as if
An exclamation point, he signifies
His stance somewhere between the hippogriff
And unicorn. He too is counterwise.
Encumbered with rare hazards, how a myth
May tower! Flesh and hides and ivories
        May doom the lesser herds; unsafe, aloof,
        Standoffishness will kill the buff giraffe.

The Vole

In kohl mines and estaminets of gold,
In loamy bushels lies the lightsome vole.
Most modest and most chary is his field
Endeavor, devious from mold to meal,
From wold to gloomy welkin. Roots uphold
His larval weather, cotyledons spill,
Seeds sound. He is at home in this moot world
Of metamorphosis. I would as well.
Adaptability I could not wield
So deftly in an equal domicile.
From sun to shade, from surfaces to sealed
And secret rooms, we'd differ: he would kill
        The interloper if he could, and build
        A perfect freedom, though all else were foiled.

The Cat and the Bird

Each day the string that joined their natural selves
Was shortened: her craving grew like a maltese tree
In which he hopped less free, less free.

O you lovely coq au vin, she all but said.
And relishing afar its sauces and its condiment,
She set the grassy tables of her restaurant.

He flew his errands out — nest-patching, food,
And evensong, not entirely independent — paired
With the haunting shadow of her hunger's tireless bird.

She in her devious den made a domesticity
Of waiting, eating an occasional canape,
Doing the wash, all with one eye up the chimney.

Less far, less far, he flew, as though her mouth were hearth
That hailed him to its summery smother:
How lovingly it licked at his ingenuous chatter.

Until, one early day in June, divining worms,
He worked his marginal milligrams too close,
And fell into her ready knives and forks.

Flight and song and all she finished secretly and neatly;
And with his toothpick bones arranged an epitaph:
Here was a bird who sang the limitless expanses of a table-
    cloth.

MARVIN SOLOMON, *born in Baltimore, Md., in 1923, lives in the town of his birth, where he is employed by a department store as a display assistant. His poems have been published in many magazines, most recently in* Paris Review *and* New Orleans Poetry Journal. *His book,* First Poems, *was published in 1952.*

WILLIAM STAFFORD

Testimony to an Inquisitor

Mud through my toes I'm from this land,
viewing it evenings from the horse trough,
meditating it through hushed hours in the morning.
I know it produces wheat and oak trees and poison ivy
and mountain parks that stab the vacationing clerk.
Its people are my people—I shrug the way they do.
On miles of street it is easy to swim their faces,
or to challenge one. Glimpsed
through doorways, the bartender is my brother;
the hootchy girl twitches for me; the Senator
grows my same kind of petunias.
I feel secure even being robbed by these people.

And you, sir, measuring me for a foreign suit—
I used to meet you every summer:
boyhood's benevolent monster that lurked
in dog days, hiding behind moss in the slough.
One year you turned out to be a rubber tire,
a great foreign-eyed white sidewall.

The more suspicious you are, the longer I've known you.

On Being Invited to a Testimonial Dinner

We are trained and quiet intellectuals
who learn all mazes very well
and in the dusk we live in go
around the room and part way up the walls.

If there is a way around, we flow;
if there is no way, then our heads know.
Blundering types who push we can forgive,
being sure that such and such makes a so-and-so,

But no man—forceful or not—can live
with credit in our minds at all till we've
checked what he is against all his pretenses,
and no forceful man commands our love.

Now, the power in thought lives by surprise.
A heart may feel beforehand; it decides
whatever way it wishes. But a head
may change in the midst of kings, to stay wise.

There was once in the jungle a feast where great men fed.
The cobra—sought to hold on his still head
the ark of dignity for all the kings, whereby
with his assurance their great worth was held—

Returned regrets: "I can't accept," was his reply,
"for my head lives by freedom, low or high,
and though my heart acts tame in the midst of kings,
my head may twitch for itself, and those kings die."

Outside

The least little sound sets the coyotes walking,
walking the edge of our comfortable earth.
We look inward, but all of them
are looking toward us as they walk the earth.

We need to let animals loose in our houses,
the wolf to escape with a pan in his mouth
and streams of animals toward the horizon
each carrying what will fit in his mouth.

All we have taken into our houses
and polished with our hands belongs to a truth
greater than ours, in the animals' keeping.
Coyotes are circling around our truth.

WILLIAM STAFFORD, *born in Kansas, grew up there, and took his earlier college work in the University of Kansas. Subsequently, he received his Ph.D. in Creative Writing from the State University of Iowa, and has worked for the U. S. Forest Service, and Church World Service. Poems by him have appeared during the fifties in many magazines. At present he teaches in Lewis and Clark College in Portland, Ore.*

MAY SWENSON

Sunday in the Country

No wind-wakeness here. A cricket's creed
intoned to the attentive wood all day.
The sun's incessant blessing. Too much gold
weighs on my head where I lay it in light.
Angels climb through my lashes, their wings
so white, every color clings there. Sky,
deep and accusing in its blue, scrapes
my conscience like a nail. I'm glad
for the gray spider who, with torpid
menace, mounts my shoe; for the skittish
fly with his green rear and orange eyes,
who wades in hairs of my arm to tickle
his belly. Long grass, silky as a monk's
beard, the blades all yellow-beamed.
Corporeal self's too shapeful for this manger.
I'm mesmerized by trumpet sun
funneling hallelujah to my veins.

Until, at the tabernacle's back, a blurt
guffaw is heard. An atheistic stranger calls
a shocking word. That wakes the insurrection!
Wind starts in the wood, and strips the pompous
cassocks from the pines. A black and
impudent Voltairean crow has spoiled
the sacrament. And I can rise and go.

To the Shore

Wheels flee on silky steel. We are seated
in a glass tube that, bullet-headed, cleaves
the scene, tossing a froth of fields and trees
and billowing land alongside.

Paced by idle clouds, we glide on a ruled diameter
of green. Preserved from weather, tidy, on display,
we are chosen fruits in a jar. But soon, the far

149

and faded hills become particular as technicolor;
too quickly the sea sparkles between them. The wide,
rough, plough-measured miles are belittled to a park.

In our space-splitting capsule where the horses
are diesel, time and the sun's heat suddenly seem
indecently excluded, along with natural grime.
Not special plums or pears, wearing blue ribbons
for county fairs, no rare aristocrats of pleasure,
we rompers to a popular shore arrive
only a little chosen above the poor. Below our
shelf of glass, cows brazenly chew, unamazed,
as we pass, and scornfully ogle our wheels,
their boredom real, and reassuring.

The Centaur

The summer that I was ten—
Can it be there was only one
summer that I was ten? It must

have been a long one then—
each day I'd go out to choose
a fresh horse from my stable

which was a willow grove
down by the old canal.
I'd go on my two bare feet.

But when, with my brother's jack-knife,
I had cut me a long limber horse
with a good thick knob for a head,

and peeled him slick and clean
except a few leaves for the tail,
and cinched my brother's belt

around his head for a rein,
I'd straddle and canter him fast
up the grass bank to the path,

trot along in the lovely dust
that talcumed over his hoofs,
hiding my toes, and turning

150

his feet to swift half-moons.
The willow knob with the strap
jouncing between my thighs

was the pommel and yet the poll
of my nickering pony's head.
My head and my neck were mine,

yet they were shaped like a horse.
My hair flopped to the side
like the mane of a horse in the wind.

My forelock swung in my eyes,
my neck arched and I snorted.
I shied and skittered and reared,

stopped and raised my knees,
pawed at the ground and quivered.
My teeth bared as we wheeled

and swished through the dust again.
I was the horse and the rider,
and the leather I slapped to his rump

spanked my own behind.
Doubled, my two hoofs beat
a gallop along the bank,

the wind twanged in my mane,
my mouth squared to the bit.
And yet I sat on my steed

quiet, negligent riding,
my toes standing the stirrups,
my thighs hugging his ribs.

At a walk we drew up to the porch.
I tethered him to a paling.
Dismounting, I smoothed my skirt

and entered the dusky hall.
My feet on the clean linoleum
left ghostly toes in the hall.

Where have you been? said my mother.
Been riding, I said from the sink,
and filled me a glass of water.

What's that in your pocket? she said.
Just my knife. It weighted my pocket
and stretched my dress awry.

Go tie back your hair, said my mother,
and *Why is your mouth all green?*
*Rob Roy, he pulled some clover
as we crossed the field,* I told her.

MAY SWENSON, *born in Logan, Utah, received her Bachelor's
degree at the state college there, and now lives in New York.
Poetry and prose by Miss Swenson have appeared in many
periodicals, including* Accent, The Nation, New World Writing,
The New Yorker, *and* Partisan Review. *Her book,* Another
Animal: Poems, *was published in* Poets of Today I, *issued in
1954. Miss Swenson received a Rockefeller Grant for creative
writing in 1955, and was awarded the Robert Frost Fellowship
in Poetry at Bread Loaf for 1957.*

MARK VAN DOREN

Comedy

The world will not be understood.
Put on a sword, put on a hood.
Listen. Can you hear me? Good.
The world will not be understood.

Tragedy

The world is something I must try,
However hard, however high.
Though I stumble, though I die,
The world is something I must try.

Tourist

I passed Olympus in the night,
But had I passed by day
I still could tell you less of it
Than blind Homer may.

Morning Worship

I wake and hear it raining.
Were I dead, what would I give
Lazily to lie here,
Like this, and live?

Or better yet: birdsong,
Brightening and spreading—
How far would I come then
To be at the world's wedding?

Now that I lie, though,
Listening, living,
(Oh, but not forever,
Oh, end arriving)

How shall I praise them:
All the sweet beings
Eternally that outlive
Me and my dying?

Mountains, I mean; wind, water, air;
Grass, and huge trees; clouds, flowers,
And thunder, and night.

Turtles, I mean, and toads; hawks, herons, owls;
Graveyards, and towns, and trout; roads, gardens,
Red berries, and deer.

Lightning, I mean, and eagles; fences; snow;
Sunrise, and ferns; waterfalls, serpents,
Green islands, and sleep.

Horses, I mean; butterflies, whales;
Mosses, and stars; and gravelly
Rivers, and fruit.

Oceans, I mean; black valleys; corn;
Brambles, and cliffs; rock, dirt, dust, ice;
And warnings of flood.

How shall I name them?
And in what order?
Each would be first.
Omission is murder.

Maidens, I mean, and apples; needles; leaves;
Worms, and planets, and clover; whirlwinds, dew;
Bulls; geese—

Stop. Lie still.
You will never be done.
Leave them all there,
Old lover. Live on.

MARK VAN DOREN *was born in Illinois in 1894. His first published book of poems was* Spring Thunder, *in 1924; his latest,* Selected Poems, *1954. In 1940 he won the Pulitzer Prize with his* Collected Poems. *He is at present a teacher in Columbia University.*

DAVID WAGONER

Gift of a Mirror to a Lady

Take it, my dear. Keep it beneath your pillow,
Beneath the flax and feathers—all the uprooted—
Beneath the hair, the bone, the dream gone yellow.
But use it someday. See what you have hated.

Lift it. You will remember by this token
The landscape where our summer turned to fable:
There lies the larchtree with its crested lichen
And, past the gate, the wet scythe and the stubble.

Close to your eyelid, see the grapevine slacken
And die, the trellis alter; there in the silvered
Flatness of your mind, the earth will sicken,
Water be silent in the moss-filled culvert.

And birds you have never seen, gold-clawed and burning,
Will splash from the fallen branches, rise to flutter
The glass beside you, striking the air and staring.
Then shatter the mirror. It was made to shatter.

"Tan Ta Ra, cries Mars . . ."
—Thomas Weelkes

"Clang!" goes the high-framed, feather-tufted gong. The
   mace
And halberd, jostled together, ring on the cobblestones;
While straight with the horde, blue flies and pieces of wings
Sail to the war. Owl's egg in mouth, the prophet sings
Glory from thumb-stirred entrails, glory from eagle-stains
And smoke, holding a cup of moly to his face.

"Blat!" go the thin-stemmed silver horns. High-tail and
   horse-behind,
Prouder than bustles, rise in the streets to prank
And fidget with the air. See, plumes at their ears,
The unicorns stumble—the ram-horned bugbears,
And the spears, all brassily crested, rank on jackstraw rank,
And the phalanx of bellies, and the rusty, bellying wind.

"Tan Ta Ra!" cries Mars, last in the callithumpian line,
Where midgets, riding on dogs, squeak like his chariot wheels

155

And weep. Ta Ra to his majesty's knotted thighs and fists!
The knuckle-browed, crotch-guarded master of hosts,
The raggedy-hafted Mars goes forth, with stars on his heels,
To battle, twitching our dust behind him like a gown.

News from the Court

Summoned by love and heat and God knows what,
On the plush-filled stairway, raising his plushy feet
(Silent, his lips as purple as his robes),
The King climbs to the Queen by candlelight.

Before his knees have knocked at the outer door,
Before his voice has lifted like a latch,
Before the ring-led fingers of the King
Have found bed-curtains flapping at a touch,

The news is trumped abroad through corridors
To the streets and sticks, earholes and buttresses,
From cup to spigot, rake to gutterstone,
And along the chancel through the bishop's nose:

Will it be prince, or princess, or still-birth?
What's the most regal answer to a bite?
How many fathoms deep is mother-of-pearl?
If the watchman says, "Ahem!" how goes the night?

But secret in state, themselves conspirators,
Ageless Regina and the First of Shades
(The King without the knavery of his lords,
The Queen without lip-service from her maids)

Perform once more their ceremonious love
For love, for time, for rage they have never lost,
He riding on her field of the cloth of gold,
She striking again the history of his breast,

And the royal couple lie in a chronicle—
Despite the clucks and pennysheets in the town—
Strewn through each other like their images:
The orb, the sceptre, and the whirling crown.

DAVID WAGONER *teaches English at the University of Washington. Indiana University Press published his first collection of poetry,* Dry Sun, Dry Wind, *in 1953, and will publish his second,* A Place to Stand, *in 1958.*

ELEANOR GLENN WALLIS

Iulus

Never had child a more adventurous life
Than young Iulus, fled from vanquished Troy's
Burnt palaces, her ruined shrines, the noise
of Greek and Trojan, loud in barbarous strife.

He went a child, his father's hand held fast:
Maturity was quick; the fickle wave
Taught him distrust of Neptune and the cave
Where man-eating Cyclops made repast.

Even the innocent meadows were a snare:
To these the wingéd Harpies might descend,
Those girl-faced vultures, quick to foul and rend
Whatever meat the Trojan could prepare.

Iulus, toughened by ferocious odds,
Gained manhood early yet was still the child
About whose hair the holy fire ran wild
In token of his favor with the gods.

Yet cool rebuke was not unknown to him:
He earned Apollo's censure for a word
Too rashly spoken or too often heard
On matters where his knowledge was but slim.

Woodcraft he used: beside the pole or net,
Skill with a bow and arrow brought him game.
He neither knew the stag he pierced was tame
Nor what a blaze his feat of arms would set.

His thoughtless shaft precipitating war,
Iulus saw the Latin city burn
And watched as fallen warriors, each in turn,
Became a stillness at the whirlwind's core.

In a City Square

Children model the dust
Since build they must,
Patting what they devise
To ant-hill size.

These molds of no renown
Are trodden down
Nor wait as sand must wait
A fluid fate.

But whether on the beach
Or here in easier reach
The restless childish hand
Builds dust or sand.

The Hunter

White as the great white dusk through which he moves,
Silent as arctic snows,
The owl traverses winter solitude
Above the floes;
And smaller creatures than himself contract,
Numb in a glaze of fear
As the voracious beak, the claw's impact
Draw near.

ELEANOR GLENN *(Mrs. Hayward)* WALLIS *was born in Baltimore, Md., where she still lives. She has published several books of poetry, the latest being* Design for an Arras, *and has won awards from* Voices, Wings, Contemporary Poetry, *and the Poetry Society of Georgia.*

CHARLES DAVID WEBB

Monasteries

That old monk confined in his cell
And I in my many
Have heard through our cork-lined wall
The clang of the morning bell

Calling the holy to prayer.
In the dim cathedral
Where the colored light
Filters to the third stair,

There that old friar
Knows the father and the son.
I know only the third light
And the human choir;

But I have heard a madrigal
Echo from that cathedral wall,
And the melody I heard
Would surely appal

This holy man—yet the chord
Blended the same:
He with his one lord
And I with my many.

Threshold

Who is waiting at the doorstep now?
The dark has not yet come.
Though sure dead leaves are soon to fall,
The dark has not yet come.

Like Laertes' our sad voices cry
Hold off the earth a while.
Though now there is no eastern light,
Dark has not yet come.

Cyrano waits by the chestnut tree;
Go to him now, Roxanne.
Quick, before the shadows cover him,
For the dark has not yet come.

Leander paces the silent shore,
Hero longs in her tower;
Neptune lurks in the hungry tide,
The dark has not yet come.

Why do we linger on the doorstep now?
Why do we linger, alone, afraid?
Dusk is spread by the chestnut tree
But dark has not yet come.

Jardin des Fleurs

Are there no roses in your garden
My young man, or have you
Looked to see? Run back now
And fall prostrate on the sod.

Have you seen your tears, like early dew,
Shape upon those petals, my young man?
They form as surely there as anywhere:
The red of blood and roses is like God,

Omnipotent, beautiful and pure.
The evil is the red will not endure.
It is not too late you know: turn back.

Solitude is not so bad if true,
Young man. I tried it once
When the world split.
I felt the dew of roses in my hair.
You try it too,
And I will join you there.

Orestes Pursued

There headlong into the calm black night,
Over a waste of thistle, sedge and briar,
A boy is running wildly towards the shore,
As if the sky itself obscured his sight;
His arms arched upward, wiry fingers tight
Around the crumpled carcass of a bird
Cold and bloody as his nettled heart,
Fraternal in the ecstasy of flight.

Run on, boy, into the gripping dark,
Until your skin is raked with thorns
And the world's blood is but a mark
On your arm. Listen to the horns
That announce morning, or the lark
That sings of it. Not sings, mourns.

And Dust to Dust

Embalming is so intricate these days
(And costly if you want the kind that stays)
That Murray Black has done the whole thing in,
Invented a quick-freeze method sure as sin
To revolutionize the trade. (Or he thinks so.)
It's a refrigerated coffin, thirty below.
Directions: slip the item in the box,
Set thermostat and automatic locks,
Put it away, forget about it. And, for free,
Murray supplies a foolproof guarantee
Of twice your money back. Lasts a lifetime too.
If uncrating seems in order, it's like new.
Inside it's lined with genuine imported kid
And a light goes on when you open the lid.
Murray will get rich on this I guess.
He always had a shrewd head for business.

CHARLES DAVID WEBB, *born near Beckley, W. Va., in 1935, has attended West Virginia University, the University of North Carolina, and the University of Toledo, where he received his B.A. in June of this year. Except for appearances in scholastic magazines, these are his first published poems.*

161

T. WEISS

The Greater Music

All things turned to Orpheus' hand.
Narcissi bloomed, and all at once,
the burning loveliness far underground,
then bloomed a retinue of bees, all hived

as in a greater self, intent on hearing
the sweetness of their lives, stilled
in that welling strain; and animals,
rapt as plungings of the sea,

admired in that pellucid glass
what they might be. But only Orpheus,
when the fierce hand plucked his strings,
could not consent to the divisions

of the lute. His breath, greeting
the stone-deaf, eager stones (though why
those fury-flying stones did not hear
and build into a tower of hearing

round his air I cannot tell), delighted
to be ript and strewn like tortured
peace out of that terrible grip,
a too rhapsodic for the mortal ear.

Yet as his head drifted down the stream,
the waters touched by that perfect lip
at once were set to dreaming, his course
the music they drank as from a golden cup.

Barracks Apt. 14

All must be used:

this clay whisky jug, bearing
a lamp-shade; the four brown pears,
lying ruggedly among each other
in the wicker basket; the cactus

in its pot; and the orange berries,
old now as they dangle from their twigs
as though badly hung there.

These as well as the silence,
the young woman reading Aristotle
with difficulty, and the little girl
in the next room, voluble in bed:
"I'm talking in my sleep . . . laughing
in my sleep . . . waking in my sleep"

all are parts hopeful, possible,
expecting their place in the song;
more appealing because parts
that must harmonize into something
that rewards them for being, rewards
with what they are.

         Do this and do,
till suddenly the scampering field
you would catch, the shiny crows
just out of reach, the pears
a russet world breaking through,
some tide invading each dry berry,
and the cactus you cannot keep
to long like that thorny Aristotle
suddenly, turning, turn on you

as meaning, the ultimate greenness
they have all the time been seeking
in the very flight they held
before you. No matter what you do,
at last you will be overwhelmed,
the distance will be broken,

    the music will confound you.

T. WEISS *was born in Reading, Pa., in 1916. He has published poetry and criticism in many leading periodicals, and is the author of one book of verse,* The Catch. *Mr. Weiss held a Ford Foundation fellowship in 1954-55 and won first prize in the Wallace Stevens awards in 1956. Editor of the* Quarterly Review of Literature, *he is Professor of Literature at Bard College.*

JOHN HALL WHEELOCK

Dialectics of Flight

To get off the ground has always been difficult
For poet or bird, and the gray gull
At the sea's edge here, who regards me with an eye
That is skeptical, shall we say, would never try
To scale heaven by direct assault—
Ascent is always oblique and casual.

But the wings must be kept ready. He stretches his wings
To keep them ready; those huge vans,
Feathered, curving forefingers, reach upward again,
Arch outward, are shaken, are slowly lowered; and then,
With curious rufflings and fidgetings,
Fold back onto the body like collapsed fans.

The sea's blue crescent, the harsh smell of the sea,
Her thunders, this perpetual roar,
These vacant beaches are background for a bird
With whom I have always wanted to have a word—
Theories of flight interest me.
I advance upon him boldly along the shore

And begin: "O master of ascent"—
When, suddenly, the great wings on either side
Canopy out; with lumbering gait he runs
Into the wind; then, all at once
(So imperceptible was the event),
Is mounted upon the wind his wings bestride.

He climbs seaward, leaving me breathless here.
Now, as he travels, gaining height,
Those two webbed feet, symbolic of his birth,
His bondage to sea and earth,
Are quietly retracted, landing gear
Needed for the interval between flight and flight.

Hippopotamothalamion

A hippopotamus had a bride
    Of rather singular beauty,
When he lay down at her side
    'Twas out of love, not duty—
    Hers was an exceptional beauty.
Take, oh take those lips away, etc.

He met her in Central Nigeria,
    While she was resident there,
Where life is distinctly superior
    And a hippo can take down her hair—
    And, God, but she was fair!
Take, oh take those lips away, etc.

She was coming up from her morning swim
    When first they chanced to meet:
He looked at her, she looked at him,
    And stood with reluctant feet
    Where mud and river meet.
Take, oh take those lips away, etc.

Their eye-beams, twisted on one thread,
    Instantaneously did twine,
And he made up poetry out of his head,
    Such as: "Dear heart, be mine"—
    And he quoted, line for line,
"Hail to thee, blithe spirit," etc.

Now, hippopotamoid courtesy
    Is strangely meticulous—
A beautiful thing, you will agree,
    In a hippopotamus—
    And she answered, briefly, thus:
"Hail to thee, blithe spirit," etc.

Perhaps she was practicing the arts
    That grace old Hippo's daughter,
The coquetries that win all hearts,
    For even as he besought her
    She slid into the water.
Out, out, brief candle, etc.

Now on the borders of the wood,
   Whence love had drawn him hither,
He paces in an anguished mood,
   Darting hither and thither
   In a terrific dither.
Out, out, brief candle, etc.

The course of true love never yet
   Ran smooth, so we are told,
With thorns its pathway is beset
   And perils manifold,
   And has been from of old.
Out, out, brief candle, etc.

Yet soon a happier morning smiles,
   The marriage feast is spread—
The flower girls were crocodiles
   When hippopotamus led
   Hippopotamus, with firm tread,
   A bride to the bridal bed.
Milton, thou should'st be living at this hour.

The Sun Men Call It

Stars have their glory and, or near or far,
Are worth our worship, as all glories are;
There is a star I worship, early and late—
The sun men call it, drinking from that great
Fountain of light, the glory of a star.

JOHN HALL WHEELOCK, *born in Far Rockaway, N. Y., in 1886, is the author of numerous books of poetry, from* The Human Fantasy, *to* Poems, Old and New. *The last item, published in 1956, won the Ridgely Torrence Memorial Award for that year. Mr. Wheelock has edited, with an introduction,* Editor to Author: The Letters of Maxwell E. Perkins; The Face of a Nation: Poetical Passages from the Writings of Thomas Wolfe; *and, since 1954, an annual volume,* Poets of Today, *presenting in one book the work of three hitherto unpublished poets. In June of this year he received an honorary L.H.D. from Otterbein College.*

Pangloss' Song

Dear boy, you will not hear me speak
With sorrow or with rancor
Of what has paled my rosy cheek
And blasted it with canker;
Twas Love, great Love, that did the deed,
Through Nature's gentle laws,
And how should ill effects proceed
From so divine a cause?

Sweet honey comes from bees that sting,
    As you are well aware.
To one adept in reasoning,
Whatever pains disease may bring
Are but the tangy seasoning
    To Love's delicious fare.

II

Columbus and his men, they say,
Conveyed the virus hither
Whereby my features rot away
And vital powers wither;
Yet had they not traversed the seas
And come infected back—
Why, think of all the luxuries
That modern life would lack!

All bitter things conduce to sweet,
    As this example shows.
Without the little spirochete,
We'd have no chocolate to eat,
Nor would tobacco's fragrance greet
    The European nose.

III

Each nation guards its native land
With cannon and with sentry;
Inspectors look for contraband
At every port of entry;

Yet nothing can prevent the spread
Of Love's divine disease;
It rounds the world from bed to bed,
As pretty as you please.

Men worship Venus everywhere,
    As plainly may be seen.
Her decorations, which I bear,
Are nobler than the *croix de guerre,*
And gained in service of our fair
    And universal Queen.

Two Voices in a Meadow

A Milkweed

Anonymous as cherubs
Over the crib of God,
White seeds are floating
Out of my burst pod.
What power had I
Before I learnt to yield?
Shatter me, great wind:
I shall possess the field.

A Stone

As casual as cow-dung
Under the crib of God,
I lie where chance would have me,
Up to the ears in sod.
Why should I move? To move
Befits a light desire.
The sills of heaven would founder
Did such as I aspire.

RICHARD WILBUR *was born in New York City in 1921. His books
are* The Beautiful Changes; Ceremony and Other Poems; Poems
1943-1956; *Moliere's* Misanthrope *(translation); and* Things
of This World. *For the last-named he won both the Pulitzer
Prize and the National Book Award in 1957. He also wrote the
lyrics for the musical adaptation of* Candide *produced in New
York in 1956. He is at present teaching at Wesleyan University
in Connecticut.*

JOHN WILLIAMS

The Dead

Noon: and the gentle air. A swallow's wing
Flits in the latticed light where branches swing
Undulant shadows over graven stone,
Obscuring common names that I have known.
Pure space diminishes the quiet dead;
The fleeceless sky is more than overhead.

These are my brothers in this mounded field.
Gathered by time, now by that time annealed,
The shape of hand or face evades my sight
And trails into an artifact of night;
I think upon their death as if it were
Only a quiet pause of time's swift blur.

These dead are mine, or I could make them so;
My will might gather them into that flow
Of meaning I perceive from where I stand—
This falling leaf that curls upon the land,
Or that thin guise of shade my eyes admit,
Where death is but my fluttering dream of it,

A level dark that comes to mindless peace,
All strife contained, and joy, in balanced ease.
These were obscure in life; obscurer still
In this dispersion of my seeking will,
They lie at the ragged ends of nerve and thought:
Their death is where they are and I am not.

It is their names I see thrust in the ground;
Here is no meaning they have sought or found.
I give them to perfection and the lone
Nothingness of God. Upon this stone
Vague images of branches cross, and light
Defines an edge of shade upon my sight.

Now summer grasses spring beneath my feet.
Houses, trees, bare distances accrete
Beneath the noon-day sun. The land lies clear,

169

Bright and impassive in the drying year.
I walk where I have been. The earth is hot,
Alive beneath me with an ageless rot.

The Meaning of Violence

Passive within the heart
Our primal anger lies
And waits, secure, apart
From what it shall despise.

Mirrored upon the brain,
It is what it has lacked.
Inversion of disdain,
Equivalent to act,

It is the self's assent
Beyond the active will.
Beyond self's vanquishment
We feed upon our kill.

For My Students, Returning to College

Now cracking grass encrusts the yard
And crisp leaves slant the brittle air;
Impassive, close, the neutral sky
Engages buildings lean and spare.
The day is new and hard.

Within these rooms the truth must lie.
Immortal, of the mortal brain,
It burns inert in cold black print
And warms the lifeless grasp to gain.
The concept does not die.

Here we have come to search the gray
And sullen stubbornness of fact:
To learn that we can never sense
Or know what we can never act,
Or what we cannot say.

A History

Burney:—"How does poor Smart do, Sir; is he likely to recover?" Johnson:—"It seems as if his mind had ceased to struggle with the disease; for he grows fat upon it."

Two years the blank walls stared at him, and moved
Unhindered through his teeming eyes. Like doom,
He scratched his song into the rotted wood:
Nor pen, nor page to cheer his wasting room.

Released by shame, he prayed in godless streets
And blessed the hungry beast's untinctured soul—
And saw at last his God's dark purblind heart
In the lion's eyeball, like a wet coal.

The Skaters

Graceful and sure with youth, the skaters glide
Upon the frozen pond. Unending rings
Expand upon the ice, contract, divide,
Till motion seems the shape that movement brings,

And shape is constant in the moving blade.
Ignorant of the beauty they invent,
Confirmed in their hard strength, the youths evade
Their frail suspension on an element,

This frozen pond that glisters in the cold.
Through all the warming air they turn and spin,
And do not feel that they grow old
Above the fragile ice they scrape and thin.

The Leaf

How quiet the day is
May be seen in her eyes
Where the pool and the pool's image
Merge; the gray leaf falls
From the ruined tree,
Sought by the water.

But the water is still,
And this quiet day
Is the driest leaf of Autumn;
Contained by the pool and buoyed there,
It holds the water
All beneath,

And holds the sky,
And that blue lady
Who perceives in them—leaf,
Sky, and pool—her intricate vision
Of the quiet day.
It has become

The densest figure
In a season's keep.
So has this autumn light
Become itself, the living source
It is perceived
And entered by.

She was a lady
In the bluest gown
Of heaven, who looked and looked
At tree and leaf and the pooled sky,
That none or all
Might disappear.

JOHN WILLIAMS, *born in 1922, received his B.A. and M.A. at the University of Denver, his Ph.D. at the University of Missouri. He teaches literature and is head of the Creative Writing program at the University of Denver. His novel,* Nothing but the Night, *was published in 1948, and a volume of poetry,* The Broken Landscape, *in 1949.*

172

WILLIAM CARLOS WILLIAMS

The Intelligent Sheep-Man
and the new cars:

I'd like to
pull
the back out

and use
one of them
to take

"the girls"
to
the fairs in.

Calypso

We watched
a red rooster
with

two hens
back
of the museum

at
St. Croix
flap his

wings
zippe zappe
and crow

The Gift

As the wise men of old brought gifts
    guided by a star
        to the humble birthplace
of the god of love,
    the devils
        as an old print shows
retreated in confusion.

What could a baby know
            of gold ornaments
or frankincense and myrrh,
        of priestly robes
                and devout genuflections?

But the imagination
        knows all stories
                before they are told
and knows the truth of this one
        past all defection

The rich gifts
        so unsuitable for a child
                though devoutly proferred,
stood for all that love can bring.
        The men were old
                how could they know

of a mother's needs
        or a child's
                appetite?

But as they kneeled
        the child was fed.
                They saw it
and
        gave praise!
                A miracle

had taken place,
        hard gold to love,
a mother's milk!
        before
                their wondering eyes.

The ass brayed
        the cattle lowed.
                It was their nature.

All men by their nature give praise.
        It is all
                they can do.

The very devils

by their flight give praise.
What is death,
beside this?
Nothing. The wise men
came with gifts

and bowed down
to worship
this perfection.

To Flossie

who showed me
a bunch of garden roses
she is keeping
on ice

against an appointment
with friends
for supper
day after tomorrow

Aren't they beautiful!
You can't
smell them
because they're so cold

but aren't they—
in wax
paper for the
moment—beautiful!

Sappho, Be Comforted

There is only one love
let it be a sparrow
to hold between the breasts
greets us daily with its small cries

what does it matter?
I, we'll say, love a woman
but truth to tell
I love myself more. Sappho loves

the music of her own
songs which men seldom

175

mean to her, a lovely girl
of whom she is desperately fond:
This is myself though
my hateful mirror
shows me every day my big nose.
Men, are indifferent to me, my sweet

but I would not trade my
skill in composition
for all (a second choice) you
present for my passionate caresses.

The Children

Once in a while
we'd find a patch
of yellow violets.

Not many.
But blue, big blue
ones in

the cemetery woods!
we'd pick
bunches of *them*.

There was a family
named Foltette
a big family

with lots of
children's graves.
So we'd take

bunches of violets
and place one
on each headstone.

This Is Pioneer Weather

Me, go to Florida!
Ha ha!
At Northfield
when we were girls

we used to take
the trays
we
had in the kitchen

and sit on them
Wow!
what a thrill!
in the field

back of the
school
down hill screaming
our heads off!

WILLIAM CARLOS WILLIAMS, *born in 1883, has written short stories, novels, and an autobiography in addition to his distinguished poetry. By profession a physician, living in his native town of Rutherford, N. J., Dr. Williams holds honorary degrees from the University of Buffalo, Bard College, Rutgers, and the University of Pennsylvania. He has won many awards, the most recent being the National Book Award in 1950, the Bollingen Prize in 1952, and the Academy of American Poets Fellowship in 1957.*

SAMUEL YELLEN

Grisaille with a Spot of Red

Winter, and the sky is a land of gray fiords
Where fogs drift and clouds twist,
All hung over with smoke and mist;
And blown across, three gray rags of birds.

Hill joined to hill by rough gray solders,
Earth is all ash and iron, lead and stone;
Trees are stripped to the brittlest of bone,
And behind and within lurk dim gray hiders.

And there across the gray countryside
Coils a highway, slate on steel:
And over the gray threshold, towards the gray goal,
Flashes an auto, red as blood.

The Wood of the Self-Destroyers
Dante: *Hell*, Canto 13

We enter the dismal wood where boughs black,
Gnarled, and thorny cradle the befouled nests
From which the harpies swoop to crunch and crack
Those wretches who jump to streets, slash their wrists,
Inhale exhaust fumes, gulp the sleeping pills,
Drink the Lysol and tear their burning breasts.
Our eyes grow used: the gloom but half conceals
Those who welcome sickness, cut off an ear,
And to ease the inward sore gorge and swill;
Who waste in apathy or cynic sneer,
Always deny and in denial smart,
Subvert the self by coward lie or fear,
And solitary, crouching each apart,
Snuffle *No! No!* to proffered hand and heart.

A Time of Light, a Time of Shadow

School was out. The boys were quelling Mars with death-ray
    gun,
The girls were going to Heaven via hopscotch,
One little toddler and one dog presumed to join the fun,
And in a scientific mood I paused to watch.

The sunlight fell about them in a cataract:
If there was shadow, then the very shadow shone;
If there was substance, that substance did not reflect
The light, but let it pass through flesh and bone.

Not yet cemented by one central will,
Each childish body simply flew apart;
Legs and arms cascaded in a random spill,
And shadows had to find their way by fit and start.

It was a time of light. Disembodied ripple,
Incorporeal speed and movement thrilled the air;
A fabric without density, a purest dapple
Would leap away and leave its shadow there.

Detached, disjoined, having lost their accustomed tether,
Those shadows twitched and fluttered in bewilderment:
They needed something, if no more than a feather,
Yet had no notion where that something went.

And watching those spirits, like luminous buttercups,
Fly by and throw no darkness as they passed,
I too presumed, and tried three small self-conscious hops;
But my shadow dragged along, mine I could not cast.

And then I saw how shadow bides its time,
How the brightest transparencies will turn opaque,
Sheer speed and animation will go lame,
And heavy shadow pile up flake by flake.

SAMUEL YELLEN, *born in Vilna, Lithuania, in 1906, has con-
tributed poems, stories, and sketches to many periodicals; his
first book of poetry,* In the House and Out, and Other
Poems, *appeared in 1952. Professor of English at Indiana Uni-
versity, and editor of the Indiana University Poetry Series, Mr.
Yellen makes his home in Bloomington. A book of stories,* The
Passionate Shepherd, *is scheduled for publication this fall.*